Metaheuristics for Big Data

Metaheuristics Set

coordinated by
Nicolas Monmarché and Patrick Siarry

Volume 5

Metaheuristics for Big Data

Clarisse Dhaenens
Laetitia Jourdan

WILEY

First published 2016 in Great Britain and the United States by ISTE Ltd and John Wiley & Sons, Inc.

ISTE Ltd
27-37 St George's Road
London SW19 4EU
UK

www.iste.co.uk

John Wiley & Sons, Inc.
111 River Street
Hoboken, NJ 07030
USA

www.wiley.com

Library of Congress Control Number: 2016944993

British Library Cataloguing-in-Publication Data
A CIP record for this book is available from the British Library
ISBN 978-1-84821-806-2

Contents

Acknowledgments

This book is an overview of metaheuristics for Big Data. Hence it is based on a large literature review conducted by the authors in the Laboratory CRIStAL (Research Center in Computer Science, Signal and Automatics), University of Lille and CNRS, France and in the Lille Nord Europe Research Center of INRIA (French National Institute for Computer Science and Applied Mathematics) between 2000 and the present. We are grateful to our former and current PhD students and colleagues for all the work they have done together with us that has led to this book.

We are particularly grateful to Aymeric Blot, Fanny Dufossé, Lucien Mousin and Maxence Vandromme who read and corrected the first versions of this book. A special word of gratitude to Marie-Elénore Marmion who read carefully and commented on several chapters.

We would like to thank Nicolas Monmarché and Patrick Siarry for their proposal to write this book and for their patience! Sorry for the time we took.

Finally, we would like to thank our families for their support and love.

Clarisse DHAENENS and Laetitia JOURDAN

Introduction

Big Data: a buzzword or a real challenge?

Both answers are suitable. On the one hand, the term *Big Data* has not yet been well defined, although several attempts have been made to give it a definition. Indeed, the term *Big Data* does not have the same meaning according to the person who uses it. It could be seen as a buzzword: *everyone talks about Big Data but no one really manipulates it.*

On the other hand, the characteristics of *Big Data*, often reduced to the three "Vs" – volume, variety and velocity – introduce plenty of new technological challenges at different phases of the Big Data process. These phases are presented in a very simple way in Figure I.1.

Starting from the generation of data, its storage and management, analyses can be made to help decision-making. This process may be reiterated if additional information is required. At each phase, some important challenges arise.

Indeed, during the generation and capture of data, some challenges may be related to technological aspects that are linked to the acquisition of real-time data, for example. However, at this phase, challenges are also related to the identification of meaningful data.

The storage and management phase leads to two critical challenges: first, the infrastructures for the storage of data and its transportation; second, conceptual models to provide well-formed available data that may be used for analysis.

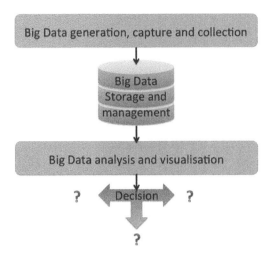

Figure I.1. *Main phases of a Big Data process*

Then, the analysis phase has its own challenges, with the manipulation of heterogeneous massive data. In particular, when considering the knowledge extraction, in which unknown patterns have to be discovered, analysis may be very complex due to the nature of data manipulated. This is at the heart of data mining. A way to address data mining problems is to model them as optimization problems. In the context of Big Data, most of these problems are large-scale ones. Hence metaheuristics seem to be good candidates to tackle them. However, as we will see in the following, metaheuristics are suitable not only to address the large size of the problem, but also to deal with other aspects of Big Data, such as variety and velocity.

The aim of this book is to present how *metaheuristics can provide answers to some of the challenges induced by the Big Data context* and particularly within the data analytics phase.

This book is composed of three parts. The first part is an introductory part consisting of three chapters. The aim of this part is to provide the reader with elements to understand the following aspects.

Chapter 1, *Optimization and Big Data*, provides elements to understand the main issues led by the *Big Data* context. It then reveals what characterizes *Big Data* and focuses on the analysis phase and, more precisely, on the data mining task. This chapter indicates how data mining problems may be seen as combinatorial optimization problems and justifies the use of metaheuristics to address some of these problems. A section is also dedicated to the performance evaluation of algorithms, as in data mining, a specific protocol has to be followed.

Chapter 2 presents an *introduction to metaheuristics*, to make this book self-contained. First, common concepts of metaheuristics are presented and then the most widely known metaheuristics are described with a distinction between single solution-based and population-based methods. A section is also dedicated to multi-objective metaheuristics, as many of them have been proposed to deal with data mining problems.

Chapter 3 provides indications on *parallel optimization* and the way metaheuristics may be parallelized to tackle very large size problems. As it will be revealed, the parallelization is considered not only to deal with large problems, but also to provide better quality solutions.

The second part, composed of the following four chapters, is the heart of the book. Each of these chapters details a data mining task and indicates how metaheuristics can be used to deal with it.

Chapter 4 begins the second part of the book and is dedicated to *clustering*. This chapter first presents the clustering task that aims to group similar objects and some of the classical approaches to solve it. Then, the chapter provides indications on the modeling of the clustering task as an optimization problem and focuses on the quality measures that are commonly used, on the interest of a multi-objective resolution approach and on the representation of a solution in metaheuristics. An overview of multi-objective methods is then proposed. The chapter ends with a specific and difficult point in the clustering task: how the estimation of the quality of a clustering solution and its validation can be done.

Chapter 5 deals with *association rules*. It first describes the corresponding data mining task and the classical approach: the *a priori* algorithm. Then, the chapter indicates how this task may be modeled as an optimization task and then focuses on metaheuristics proposed to deal with this task. It differentiates the metaheuristics according to the type of rules that are considered: categorical association rules, quantitative association rules or fuzzy association rules. A general table summarizes the most important works of the literature.

Chapter 6 is dedicated to *supervised classification*. Data mining is of great importance as it allows the prediction of the class of a new observation regarding information from observations whose classes are known. The chapter first gives a description of the classification task and briefly presents standard classification methods. Then, an optimization perspective of some of these standard methods is presented as well as the use of metaheuristics to optimize some of them. The last part of the chapter is dedicated to the use of metaheuristics for the search of classification rules, viewed as a special case of association rules.

Chapter 7 deals with *feature selection for classification* that aims to reduce the number of attributes and to improve the classification performance. The chapter uses several notions that are presented in Chapter 6 on classification. After a presentation of generalities on feature selection, the chapter gives its modeling as an optimization problem. Different representations of solutions and their associated search mechanisms are then presented. An overview of metaheuristics for feature selection is finally proposed.

Finally, *the last part* is composed of a single chapter (Chapter 8) which presents *frameworks* dedicated to data mining and/or metaheuristics. A short comparative survey is provided for each kind of framework.

Browsing the different chapters, the reader will have an overview of the way metaheuristics have been applied so far to tackle problems that are present in the Big Data context, with a focus on the data mining part, which provides the optimization community with many challenging opportunities of applications.

1

Optimization and Big Data

The term *Big Data* refers to vast amounts of information that come from different sources. Hence *Big Data* refers not only to this huge data volume but also to the diversity of data types, delivered at various speeds and frequencies. This chapter attempts to provide definitions of *Big Data*, the main challenges induced by this context, and focuses on Big Data analytics.

1.1. Context of Big Data

As depicted in Figure 1.1, the evolution of Google requests on the term "Big Data" has grown exponentially since 2011.

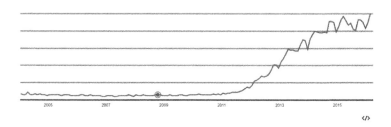

Figure 1.1. *Evolution of Google requests for "Big Data" (Google source)*

How can we explain the increasing interest in this subject? Some responses may be formulated, when we know that everyday 2.5 quintillion bytes of data are generated – such that 90% of the data in the world today have been created in the last two years. These data come from everywhere, depending on the industry and organization: sensors are used to gather climate information, posts to social media sites, digital pictures and videos, purchase transaction records and cellphone GPS signals, to name but a few [IBM 16b]. Such data are recorded, stored and analyzed.

1.1.1. *Examples of situations*

Big Data appears in a lot of situations where large amounts of complex data are generated. Each situation presents challenges to handle. We may cite some examples of such situations:

– *Social networks*: the quantity of data generated in social networks is huge. Indeed, monthly estimations indicate that 12 billion tweets are sent by about 200 million active users, 4 billion hours of video are watched on YouTube and 30 billion pieces of content are shared on Facebook [IBM 16a]. Moreover, such data are of different formats/types.

– *Traffic management*: in the context of creation of smart cities, the traffic within cities is an important issue. This becomes feasible, as the widespread adoption in recent years of technologies such as smartphones, smartcards and various sensors has made it possible to collect, store and visualize information on urban activities such as people and traffic flows. However, this also represents a huge amount of data collected that need to be managed.

– *Healthcare:* in 2011, the global size of data in healthcare was estimated as 150 exabytes. Such data are unique and difficult to deal with because: 1) data are in multiple places (different source systems in different formats including text as well as images); 2) data are structured and unstructured; 3) data may be inconsistent (they may have different definitions according to the person in charge of filling data); 4) data are complex (it is difficult to identify standard processes); 5) data are subject to regulatory requirement changes [LES 16].

– *Genomic studies:* with the rapid progress of DNA sequencing techniques that now allows us to identify more than 1 million SNPs (genetic variations), large-scale genome-wide association studies (GWAS) have become practical. The aim is to track genetic variations that may, for example, explain genetic susceptibility for a disease. In their analysis on the new challenges induced by these new massive data, Moore *et al.* first indicate the necessity of the development on new biostatistical methods for quality control, imputation and analysis issues [MOO 10]. They also indicate the challenge of recognizing the complexity of the genotype–phenotype relationship that is characterized by significant heterogeneity.

In all these contexts, the term *Big Data* is now become a widely used term. Thus, this term needs to be defined clearly. Hence, some definitions are proposed.

1.1.2. *Definitions*

Many definitions of the term *Big Data* have been proposed. Ward and Baker propose a survey on these definitions [WAR 13]. As a common aspect, all these definitions indicate that size is not the only characteristic.

A historical definition was given by Laney from Meta Group in 2001 [LAN 01]. Indeed, even if he did not mention the term "Big Data", he identified, mostly for the context of e-commerce, new data management challenges along three dimensions – the three "Vs": volume, velocity and variety:

– *Data volume:* as illustrated earlier, the number of data created and collected is huge and the growth of information size is exponential. It is estimated that 40 zettabytes (40 trillion gigabytes) will be created by 2020.

– *Data velocity:* data collected from connected devices, websites and sensors require specific data management not only because of real-time analytics needs (analysis of streaming data) but also to deal with data obtained at different speeds.

– *Data variety:* there is a variety of data coming from several types of sources. Dealing simultaneously with such different data is also a difficult challenge.

The former definition has been extended. First, a fourth "V" has been proposed: *veracity*. Indeed, another important challenge is the uncertainty of data. Hence around 1 out of 3 business leaders do not trust the information they use to make decisions [IBM 16a]. In addition, a fifth "V" may also be associated with Big Data: *value*, in a sense that the main interest to deal with data is to produce additional value from information collected [NUN 14].

More recently, following the line of "V" definitions, Laney and colleagues from Gartner [BEY 12] propose the following definition:

"Big data" is high-volume, -velocity and -variety information assets that demand cost-effective, innovative forms of information processing for enhanced insight and decision-making.

This definition has been reinforced and completed by the work of DeMauro *et al.* who analyzed recent corpus of industry and academic articles [DEM 16]. They found that the main themes of Big Data are: information, technology, methods and impact. They propose a new definition:

Big Data is the Information asset characterized by such a high-volume, -velocity and -variety to require specific technology and analytical methods for its transformation into value.

Even if these definitions of 3Vs, 4Vs or 5Vs are the more widely used to explain to a general public the context of Big Data, some other attempts of definitions have been proposed. The common point of these definitions is to mainly reduce the importance of the size characteristic for the benefit of the complexity one.

For example, in the definition proposed by MIKE2.0 [1], it is indicated that elements of *Big Data* include [MIK 15]:

– the degree of complexity within the dataset;

– the amount of value that can be derived from innovative versus non-innovative analysis techniques;

– the use of longitudinal information supplements the analysis.

They indicate that "big" refers to big complexity rather than big volume. Of course, valuable and complex datasets of this sort naturally tend to grow rapidly and so Big Data quickly becomes truly massive. *Big Data can be very small and not all large datasets are big.* As an example, they consider that the

---

1 MIKE2.0 (Method for an Integrated Knowledge Environment) is an open source delivery framework for Enterprise Information Management.

data streaming from a hundred thousand sensors on an aircraft is Big Data. However, the size of the dataset is not as large as might be expected. Even a hundred thousand sensors, each producing an eight byte reading every second, would produce less than 3GB of data in an hour of flying (100,000 sensors × 60 minutes × 60 seconds × 60 bytes).

1.1.3. *Big Data challenges*

Rather, it is a combination of data management technologies that have evolved over time. Big Data enables organizations to store, manage and manipulate vast amounts of data at the right speed and at the right time to get the right insights.

Hence the different steps of the value chain of *Big Data* may be organized in three stages:

1) data generation and acquisition;

2) data storage and management;

3) data analysis.

Each of these stages leads to challenges from the highest importance. Many books and articles are dedicated to this subject (see, for example, [CHE 14, HU 14, JAG 14]).

1.1.3.1. *(Big) Data generation and acquisition*

The generation of data is not a problem anymore, due to the huge number of sources that can generate data. We may cite all kinds of sensors, customer purchasing, astronomical data and text messages. One of the challenges may be to *a priori* identify data that may be interesting to generate. What should be measured? This is directly linked with the analysis that needs to be realized. Much of these data, for example data generated by sensor networks that are highly redundant, can be filtered and compressed by orders of magnitude without compromising our ability to reason about the underlying activity of interest. One challenge is to define these *online* filters in such a way that they do not discard useful information, since the raw data is often too voluminous to even allow the option of storing it all [JAG 14]. On the contrary, generated data may offer a rich context for further analysis (but may lead to very complex ones).

Before being stored, an information extraction process that extracts the required information from the underlying sources and expresses it in a structured form suitable for storage and analysis is required. Indeed, most data sources are notoriously unreliable: sensors can be faulty, humans may provide biased opinions, remote websites might be stale and so on. Understanding and modeling these sources of error is a first step toward developing data cleaning techniques. Unfortunately, much of this is data source and application dependent and is still a technical challenge [JAG 14].

1.1.3.2. *(Big) Data storage and management*

Many companies use one or several relational database management systems to store their data. This allows them to identify what the data stored are and where they are stored. However, these systems are less adapted for a Big Data context and one of the challenges linked to Big Data is the development of efficient technologies to store available data.

These technologies must be able to deal with specificities of Big Data, such as scalability (limitations of the underlying physical infrastructure), variety of data (including unstructured data), velocity of data (taking into account non-synchronous acquisition), etc. Hence, non-relational database technologies, such as NoSQL, have been developed. These technologies do not rely on tables and may be more flexible.

Among these technologies, we may cite:

– key-value pair databases, based on the key-value pair model, where most of the data are stored as strings;

– document databases, a repository for full document-style content. In addition, the structure of the documents and their parts may be provided by JavaScript Object Notation (JSON) and/or Binary JSON (BSON);

– columnar databases or column-oriented database, where data are stored in across rows (e.g. HBase from Apache). This offers great flexibility, performance and scalability, in terms of volume and variety of data;

– graph databases, based on node relationships that have been proposed to deal with highly interconnected data;

– spatial databases that incorporate spatial data. Let us note that spatial data itself is standardized through the efforts of the Open Geospatial Consortium

(OGC), which establishes OpenGIS (geographic information system) and a number of other standards for spatial data.

Big Data management includes data transportation [CHE 14]: transportation of data from data sources to data centers or transportation of data within data centers. For both types of transportation, technical challenges arise:

– efficiency of the physical network infrastructure to deal with the growth of traffic demand (the physical network infrastructure in most regions around the world is constituted by high-volume, high-rate and cost-effective optic fiber transmission systems, but other technologies are under study);

– security of transmission to ensure the property of data as well as its provenance.

These technological challenges related to data acquisition, storage and management are crucial to obtain well-formed available data that may be used for analysis.

1.1.3.3. *(Big) Data analysis*

(Big) Data analysis aims at extracting knowledge from the data. Regarding the knowledge to be extracted, Maimon *et al.* identify three levels of analysis [MAI 07]:

– *Reports:* the simplest level deals with report generation. This may be obtained by descriptive statistics as well as simple database queries.

– *Multi-level analysis:* this requires advanced database organization to make such analysis (OLAP multi-level analysis).

– *Complex analysis:* this is used to discover unknown patterns. This concerns specifically data mining, as it will be defined later, and requires efficient approaches. This book focuses on this level of analysis.

In contrast to traditional data, Big Data varies in terms of volume, variety, velocity, veracity and value. Thus, it becomes difficult to analyze Big Data with traditional data analytics tools that are not designed for them. Developing adequate Big Data analytics techniques may help discover more valuable information. Let us note that *Big Data* brings not only new challenges, but also opportunities – the interconnected Big Data with complex and heterogeneous contents bear new sources of knowledge and insights.

We can observe that while *Big Data* has become a highlighted buzzword over the last few years, *Big Data mining*, i.e. mining from Big Data, has almost immediately followed up as an emerging interrelated research area [CHE 13].

Typically, the aim of data mining is to uncover interesting patterns and relationships hidden in a large volume of raw data. Applying existing data mining algorithms and techniques to real-world problems has recently been running into many challenges. Current data mining techniques and algorithms are not ready to meet the new challenges of Big Data. Mining Big Data requires highly scalable strategies and algorithms, more efficient preprocessing steps such as data filtering and integration, advanced parallel computing environments, and intelligent and effective user interaction.

Hence the goals of Big Data mining techniques go beyond fetching the requested information or even uncovering some hidden relationships and patterns between numerous parameters. Analyzing fast and massive stream data may lead to new valuable insights and theoretical concepts [CHE 13]. In particular, the need for designing and implementing very-large-scale parallel machine learning and data mining algorithms (ML-DM) has increased remarkably, parallel to the emergence of powerful parallel and very-large-scale data processing platforms, e.g. Hadoop MapReduce [LAN 15].

In this book, we are mainly interested in this stage of the value chain of *Big Data*, that is to say how can we analyze Big Data and, in particular, how metaheuristics may be used for this. Hence the analysis stage is detailed in the following sections.

1.1.4. *Metaheuristics and Big Data*

A common definition of metaheuristics is:

Techniques and methods used for solving various optimization problems, especially large-scale ones.

By this definition, metaheuristics seem to be good candidates to solve large-scale problems induced by the *Big Data* context.

However, metaheuristics are able to provide the answer not only to the large-scale characteristics, but also to the other ones:

– *Data volume:* metaheuristics are mostly developed for large-scale problems. Moreover, their ability to be parallelized gives opportunities to deal with very large ones.

– *Data velocity:* in a context where data are regularly updated and/or the response must be a real-time one, metaheuristics are any-time methods that may propose a good solution rapidly (even if it is not optimal).

– *Data variety:* working simultaneously with different types of data may be difficult for some standard methods, for example those coming from statistics. Metaheuristics propose encodings that are able to consider several types of data simultaneously. This will give the opportunity to jointly analyze data coming from different sources.

– *Data veracity:* working with uncertainty (or more precisely with unknown data) may also be difficult for classical methods. Metaheuristics can propose to integrate stochastic approaches or partial analysis to be able to extract information from these non-precise data.

– *Data value:* metaheuristics are optimization methods based on an objective function. Hence they enable us to evaluate the interest of the knowledge extracted, its value. Using different objective functions gives the opportunity to express the value in different ways according to the context to which it is applied, for example.

In the context of Big Data, metaheuristics have mostly been used within the data analysis step for solving data mining tasks. However, some of them have been proposed to solve other kinds of optimization problems that are related to the Big Data context.

For example, in the work of Stanimirovic and Miskovic, a problem of exploration of online social networks is studied [STA 13]. The goal is to choose locations for installing some control devices and to assign users to active control devices. Several objective functions are proposed. They formulate the problems as several optimization problems and propose a metaheuristic (a pure evolutionary algorithm; EA) and two hybrid metaheuristics (EA with a local search; EA with a Tabu Search) to solve the identified optimization problems (for more information about metaheuristics, see Chapter 2). Therefore, they define all the necessary components (encodings, operators, etc.). They compare their methods on large-scale problems (up to 20,000 user nodes and 500 potential locations) in terms of quality of the solution produced and time required to obtain a good solution. The results obtained are very convincing.

1.2. Knowledge discovery in Big Data

The relationships between metaheuristics and Big Data are linked strongly to the data analysis step, which consists of extracting knowledge from available data. Hence we will focus on this data mining aspect. This section will first situate the data mining in the whole context of knowledge discovery and then present the main data mining tasks briefly. These tasks will be discussed in detail in the following chapters of the book, as one chapter will be dedicated to each of them. Hence, each chapter will present an optimization point of view of the data mining task concerned and will present how metaheuristics have been used to deal with it.

1.2.1. *Data mining versus knowledge discovery*

Knowledge Discovery in Databases (KDD) has recently seen an explosion of interest in many application domains, thanks to the numerous data available that have to be deeply analyzed not only with simple reporting. KDD is the process of identifying valid, novel, useful and understandable patterns from large datasets. Data mining (DM) is the mathematical core of the KDD process, involving the inferring algorithms that explore the data, develop mathematical models and discover significant patterns (implicit or explicit) – which are the essence of valuable knowledge [MAI 10].

Hence KDD is an inductive (not deductive) process. Its aim is to infer knowledge that is generalized from the data in the database. This process is generally not supported by classical database manager systems.

Knowledge discovery problems raise interesting challenges for several research domains such as statistics, information theory, databases, machine learning, data visualization and also for operations research (OR) and optimization as very large search spaces of solutions have to be explored.

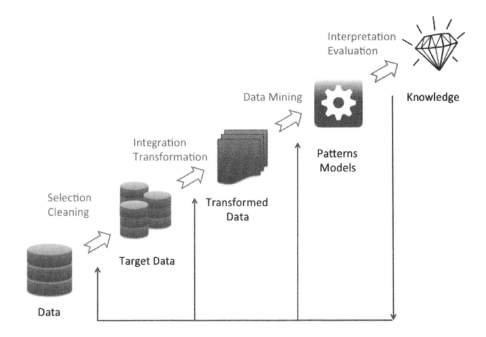

Figure 1.2. *Overview of the KDD process*

Given a context and intended knowledge that has to be extracted (that may be expressed by questions), a KDD project is identified. Then, the whole KDD process starts from raw data and applies different steps to produce knowledge from this data (see Figure 1.2):

– *Selection/cleaning:* starting from raw data, some information is selected to deal with the KDD goals that are identified. Then, the cleaning step may consist of handling missing values and removing noise or outliers, for example. Complex statistical methods as well as data mining algorithms have been proposed for this purpose. This is a crucial step as these data represent the raw material for the following steps.

– *Integration/transformation:* the aim of this second step is to prepare data to be exploited. It may include dimension reduction (feature selection, sampling) and attribute transformation (discretization of numerical attributes and functional transformation). This may also be a crucial step for the success of the KDD project as it is context dependent and is directly linked to the goals of the KDD project.

– *Data mining:* this is the heart of the knowledge discovery process. It allows the extraction of useful information from large datasets or databases. Several data mining tasks may be identified according to the type of patterns expected. Within this data mining step, which can be iterative, an important aspect deals with the evaluation of the extracted patterns. This data mining step is described hereafter.

– *Interpretation/evaluation:* patterns extracted from the data mining step are transformed into knowledge, thanks to interpretation. An evaluation is realized to determine whether the extracted knowledge has a real value (this is a new knowledge) and whether it answers the identified goals. If not, some adjustments have to be done and the process is reiterated either from the beginning or from an intermediate step.

1.2.2. *Main data mining tasks*

Data mining tasks can be classified into two categories: predictive or supervised and descriptive or unsupervised tasks. The supervised tasks learn on available data to make predictions for new data, whereas unsupervised tasks involve a description of the data and existing relationships. Main data mining tasks are (supervised) classification, clustering (also called unsupervised classification), association rule mining and feature selection, as depicted in Figure 1.3. Indeed, even if the feature selection may be used in the integration step, to prepare data, it can also be jointly used with other data mining tasks such as classification or clustering. Hence we decide to consider it within data mining tasks. To give a general overview, each of these tasks is briefly described hereafter. They will be detailed in the chapters dedicated to them.

1.2.2.1. *(Supervised) classification and regression*

The aim is to build a model to predict the unknown value of a target variable from the known values of other variables. In a classification problem, the variable being predicted, called the class, is categorical and the task becomes a regression problem when the predicted variable is quantitative. The model is constructed using available data (available observations), and then for new observations, the model is applied to determine the value of the target variable.

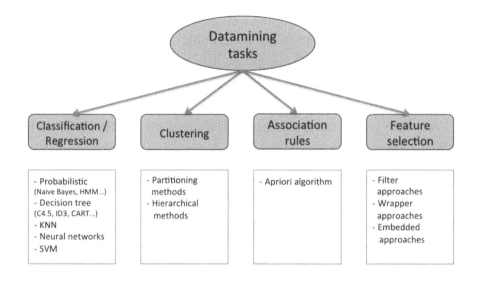

Figure 1.3. *Overview of main tasks and approaches in data mining*

There are numerous applications of classification. It can be used, for example:

– in fraud detection, to determine whether a particular credit card transaction is fraudulent;

– in medical disease diagnosis, to determine whether a patient may pick up a disease in the future;

– in marketing, to identify customers who may be interested in a given product;

– in social network analysis, to predict useful properties of actors in a social network.

Several approaches have been proposed. For an overview on Big Data classification, the reader may refer to [SUT 15]. Among the most widely used approaches, we may cite:

– *Probabilistic classification:* this uses statistical inference to compute a probability of an observation to belong to each of the possible class. The class with the highest probability is selected as the best class. Such an approach allows the computation of confidence value associated with its selected class label. Classical models and algorithms for probabilistic classification include Naive Bayes classifier, logistic regression, HMM, etc.

– *Decision trees* create a hierarchical partitioning of the data using a split criterion. Some of the methods for decision tree construction are C4.5, ID3 and CART.

– The *KNN (K-nearest neighbors)* method associates each new observation with the most represented class within its K-nearest neighbors. This method does not require any learning phase. To deal with data in a Big Data context, a MapReduce-based framework to distribute the partitioning methodology for prototype reduction techniques has been proposed [TRI 15].

– *Neural networks* simulate the human brain and its ability to perform learning.

– *SVM classifiers* use a linear condition to separate the classes from one another. Recently, an implementation of SVM on a quantum computer has been proposed to deal with very large size datasets [REB 13].

1.2.2.2. *Unsupervised classification or clustering*

The clustering task aims at decomposing or partitioning a dataset into groups so that points (here the observations) in a group are similar to each other (distance between points of the groups is minimized) and are as different as possible from points of other groups (distance between points of different groups is maximized). Clustering is directly linked to the definition of a distance between points.

The main classical approaches for clustering are:

– *partitioning methods* partition data into sets so that sets are as homogeneous as possible. The most famous method is k-means;

– *hierarchical methods* either merge or divide clusters to construct homogeneous ones.

Within the clustering task, we may also consider the *biclustering*, co-clustering or two-mode clustering that simultaneously cluster rows and columns of the matrix representing data [MIR 96, KRI 09]. This subspace clustering allows us to treat attributes and objects interchangeably, and to find relationships between elements with regard to these two directions. Different types of biclusters may be required: either biclusters with constant values, or constant values on lines or columns, or biclusters with coherent additive or multiplicative values. These approaches have been widely used in bioinformatics and many algorithms, mainly based on statistics, have been proposed. The complexity of biclustering problems depends on the exact formulation of the problem, but most of them are $\mathcal{NP}$-complete, which limits the use of exact approaches for large-scale problems.

1.2.2.3. *Association rule mining*

The association rules problem was first formulated by Agrawal *et al.* [AGR 93] and was called the market-basket problem. The initial formulation of this problem was: given a set of items and a large collection of sales records – a transaction date and a list of items bought in the transaction – the task is to find relationships between the items contained in the different transactions. Since this first application, many other problems have been studied with association rules that are defined in a more general way. Let us consider a database composed of transactions (records) described according to several – maybe many – attributes (columns). Association rules provide a very simple (but useful) way to present correlations or other relationships among attributes expressed in the form $A \Rightarrow C$, where A is the antecedent part (condition) and C the consequent part (prediction). A and C are sets of attributes that are disjoint. The best-known algorithm to mine association rules was *a priori* proposed by Agrawal and Srikant [AGR 94]. This two-phase algorithm first finds all frequent item sets and then generates high confidence rules from these sets. A lot of improvements of the initial method, as well as efficient implementations (including parallel implementations), have been proposed to enable us to deal with very large databases [BOR 03, YE 06, ZAK 01].

1.2.2.4. *Feature selection*

A difficulty in data mining is linked to the huge size of datasets and the presence of too many attributes. Including all the attributes could lead to a worse model in the classification procedure than if some of them were removed. For example, some attributes could be redundant or unrelated to the predictor variable. Hence the selection of some attributes could be necessary to reduce the computational time of data mining algorithms, to simplify the model obtained to have an accurate discrimination between observations. Then, the objective is to find a subset of p' relevant variables, where $p' << p$.

Therefore, the main goal of feature selection in supervised learning is to find a feature subset that produces higher classification accuracy. On the other hand, in unsupervised learning, feature selection aims to find a good subset of features that forms high-quality clusters for a given number of clusters.

In supervised learning, three approaches exist according to the interaction with the classification procedure:

– *filter approaches* evaluate features according to their characteristics to select (or not) them;

– *wrapper approaches* evaluate the quality of a subset of features using a learning algorithm, for example;

– *embedded approaches* combine the two aforementioned approaches by incorporating in a wrapper approach a deeper interaction between attribute selection and classifier construction.

1.2.3. *Data mining tasks as optimization problems*

As discussed previously, data mining tasks deal with operations such as the affectation of an object to a class, the grouping of objects, the selection of features, etc. All of these problems may be formulated as combinatorial optimization problems. Hence several works using optimization methods to solve data mining problems have been proposed [KAR 06, OLA 06, OLA 08, MEI 10, COR 12].

The context of Big Data makes difficult to solve those problems using exact approaches. Hence metaheuristics will be an interesting answer. In their book, Maimon *et al.* focus on soft computing for knowledge discovery. Although the chapters in that book present various approaches, the majority relate to metaheuristics, particularly evolutionary algorithms and swarm intelligence [MAI 07]. Moreover, Freitas focuses in his book on data mining and knowledge discovery with evolutionary algorithms, which represent one part of metaheuristics [FRE 08, FRE 13]. In particular, this book reveals how evolutionary algorithms may also be used for data preparation, rule discovery (included fuzzy rules) or clustering. Let us remark that one chapter is dedicated to the scaling of such algorithms to deal with large datasets.

1.3. Performance analysis of data mining algorithms

1.3.1. *Context*

There is no consensus on how to define and measure the quality of the extracted knowledge. However, three important properties may be mentioned: an extracted knowledge must be accurate, comprehensible and interesting [FRE 13]. The relative importance of these three aspects is highly dependent on the application context and must be defined at the beginning of the KDD process. In the same manner, the way of measuring each of these properties may also vary from one application context to another.

We consider in this part that the quality measure has been determined, and we focus on the methodology used to evaluate the performance of algorithms (which may be stochastic algorithms and may require several executions) and particularly to make comparisons between each one. Difficulties in the context of data mining are of several types:

1) *learning context:* the quality of the knowledge extracted – for example, the classification model or the clusters constructed – depends on its ability to be used on future unknown data. To evaluate this ability, a specific methodology is used to divide data into data used to learn (training dataset) and data used to evaluate the quality (validation dataset);

2) *supervised/unsupervised context:* in the supervised context, the ideal solution is known and may be used for the evaluation (for example, in a classification context, classes are known and it is possible to evaluate errors made by a classification model). In the unsupervised context, no information is *a priori* known on the knowledge extracted. Hence it may be difficult to evaluate quality as no reference exists. Most of the time indicators to measure the quality are proposed;

3) *specific versus generic:* as explained before, many steps in the KDD process are problem-specific. Hence designing a data mining method that is efficient in several application contexts may be difficult (and often useless). Therefore, regarding the interest of designing specific methods or generic ones, comparisons of algorithms may be realized either on specific datasets or not. When using several types of datasets, it may then be difficult to identify a

method that outperforms the others. Statistical tests must be done to examine the efficiency of the compared approaches, as explained hereafter.

Performance analysis of data mining algorithms is also a difficult task, which may have an impact on the choice of the method to use and in turn the quality of the results obtained. However, let us recall that whatever the quality of the results obtained, ultimately, a decision maker has to interpret the results. For these reasons, no responsible user will cede authority to the computer system. Rather, the decision maker will try to understand and verify the results produced by the data mining method. The data mining method must provide efficient visualization tools to make easy to the decision maker the analysis of results. This is an additional challenge with Big Data due to its complexity [JAG 14].

1.3.2. *Evaluation among one or several dataset(s)*

Regarding whether one or several dataset(s) are used to evaluate the performance of algorithms, some statistical tests have to be conducted to determine whether algorithms reach significant performance differences. Figure 1.4 shows a methodology proposed in [JAC 13a, JAC 13b] that identifies the statistical test to use, according to the number of datasets used for the comparison and the number of algorithms compared. It can be explained as follows.

First, while evaluating algorithms that have been executed several times, producing a set of results, among a single dataset (to identify the best algorithm for it, mostly a real-life one), the statistical test to use will depend on the number of algorithms compared. If only two algorithms are compared, then the Mann–Whitney test [MAN 47] on the set of results may be used. If more than two algorithms are compared, first the Kruskal–Wallis test [KRU 52] is used to determine whether algorithms are equivalent. However, additional tests may be performed to compare algorithms pairwise (the Mann–Whitney test, for example).

While evaluating algorithms among several datasets, it is unlikely that one algorithm will outperform others in all the datasets. In the context of data mining, Demsar proposes recommendations to compare multiple learning algorithms over multiple datasets [DEM 06]. These recommendations present a way to evaluate the general performance of an algorithm over several independent datasets or problems, instead of evaluating the performance on a single one. The methodology proposed by Jacques *et al.* follows these recommendations [JAC 13a, JAC 13b]. It may be described as follows. When the number of datasets is small, the Mann–Whitney test [MAN 47] may still be used. However, as it deals with each dataset/algorithm separately, it will be less efficient when the number of datasets/algorithms increases. In this case, *Friedman* [FRI 37] and *Iman-Davenport* [IMA 80] statistical tests are used to detect differences between multiple algorithms over several datasets. These tests are based on ranks obtained by the algorithms over the different datasets. Then, the average ranks are exploited to graphically draw the results. Finally, pairwise comparison of algorithms is performed using the *Wilcoxon* statistical test [WIL 45] and the *Bergmann and Hommel's* [BER 87] procedure, as recommended by Garcia and Herrera [GAR 08].

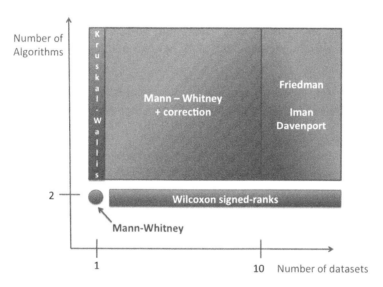

Figure 1.4. *Statistical test summary [JAC 13b]*

Following these recommendations allows us to determine whether significant differences in performance between algorithms may be found. In a Big Data context, where data may have changed over time, it is important to have a general view of the performance of the approaches used. Moreover, while applying optimization approaches and, in particular, metaheuristics that may be stochastic, a rigorous comparison approach is required.

1.3.3. *Repositories and datasets*

To compare performance of data mining approaches, classical datasets that are available on some repositories may be used. Among the most famous ones, we may cite:

– *UCI:* UC Irvine Machine Learning Repository – http://archive.ics.uci.edu/ml/ – that is the historical dataset repository. It provides 348 datasets to the machine learning community. To select datasets to use, several filters may be applied: data mining task, attribute type, data type, application area, size, etc. Let us remark that not many very large size datasets are available.

– *KDnuggets* – http://www.kdnuggets.com/datasets/ – provides links to 1) government and public data sites and portals, 2) data APIs from marketplaces, search engines, etc. and 3) data mining and data science competitions.

– *kaggle* – https://www.kaggle.com – is the leading platform for data prediction competitions and lists current data science competitions.

– *KEEL:* Knowledge Extraction based on Evolutionary Learning – http://sci2s.ugr.es/keel/ – is an open source java software for data mining and provides a dataset repository with more than 900 datasets.

– *RDataMining.com* – http://www.rdatamining.com/resources/data – provides links to other dataset repositories as well as specific tweets data (http://www.rdatamining.com/data).

– *Wikipedia* – https://en.wikipedia.org/wiki/List_of_datasets_for_machine_learning_research – provides datasets cited in peer-reviewed academic journals, ordered by applications.

Usually, the same datasets may be found on several repositories. The format of data may be different, as existing data mining frameworks have their own input formats. This will be discussed in Chapter 8, which is dedicated to frameworks.

1.4. Conclusion

Beyond the buzzword *Big Data*, real significant challenges exist. They are also linked to data acquisition, storage, management and analysis. While focusing on the analysis phase, several data mining tasks may be seen as combinatorial optimization problems and optimization approaches, and, in particular, metaheuristics have been widely used to deal with these problems. Indeed, metaheuristics are good candidates to solve large-scale problems induced by the Big Data context, as well as to deal with other characteristics such as velocity, variety, veracity or value of knowledge.

2

Metaheuristics – A Short Introduction

Knowledge discovery – particularly the data mining phase – in large databases involves the construction and evaluation of many potential explaining models. Some of these models appear to be very good predictors, whereas some of them may be very bad ones. Hence the quality of these models may be measured according to the context and the aim of the knowledge discovery process. An optimization approach would consider each model as a possible solution of the data mining problem that consists of explaining relationships between data. The quality of a solution depends on the quality of the model. Hence knowledge extraction problems can be formulated as combinatorial optimization problems and methods dedicated to these kinds of problems, such as metaheuristics, may be used.

This chapter first provides some basic information on combinatorial optimization problems and their resolution methods. The second part focuses on metaheuristics, while presenting their common concepts. The third and fourth parts present the main metaheuristics while distinguishing metaheuristics working on a single solution from metaheuristics working on populations of solutions. This presentation is illustrated by some general insights on the way to design such an approach for data mining problems. Then, the last part of the chapter provides some information about multi-objective metaheuristics.

This chapter does not pretend to present every concept concerning metaheuristics, as several books dedicated to these methods have already been published (see, for example, [GLO 03, TAL 09, GEN 10]) as well as some surveys [BLU 03, BOU 13], but basic notions necessary to understand the next chapters are presented.

2.1. Introduction

Knowledge discovery problems may be formulated as combinatorial optimization problems. In this section, an insight into such combinatorial optimization problems and the way to solve them is provided, to understand the context of using metaheuristics. Recent surveys on the use of metaheuristics, particularly evolutionary algorithms, for knowledge discovery tasks may also be interesting to consider [FRE 13, MUK 14b].

2.1.1. *Combinatorial optimization problems*

Optimization problems include a large class of problems having applications in a variety of domains. An optimization problem may be defined by:

– $\mathcal{D}$ a set of solutions that represents the decision space (also called the search space);

– f, an objective function that associates with each solution s a value (most of the time a real value) representing its quality.

A minimization problem may be defined by:

$$min f(s)$$
$$s \in \mathcal{D}$$

According to the problem, solutions $s \in \mathcal{D}$ may be of different natures and may be defined by constraints determining feasible solutions. In case of a finite set of discrete solutions $\mathcal{D}$, the problem becomes a combinatorial optimization problem. Hence, a combinatorial optimization problem consists of optimizing (minimizing or maximizing) a given objective function under a set of constraints that allows describing the set of feasible solutions. The wide variety of problems in combinatorial optimization is due to numerous applications. Indeed, combinatorial optimization problems may be found in production management, telecommunication network design, bio-informatics, scheduling and knowledge discovery, among many other tasks.

2.1.2. *Solving a combinatorial optimization problem*

Solving a combinatorial optimization problem requires three main points:

– definition of the set of feasible solutions;

– determination of the objective function to optimize;

– choice of the optimization method.

The first two points deal with the modeling of the problem, whereas the third point deals with the resolution of the problem. To define the set of feasible solutions, it is necessary to express the set of constraints of the problem that requires knowledge of the problem under study and of its application domain. Similarly, the determination of the objective function also requires knowledge of the problem, as it is necessary to be able to qualify what a good solution would be. Finally, the choice of the optimization method will often depend on the complexity of the problem. Indeed, according to its complexity, it may or not be possible to solve the problem optimally.

2.1.3. *Main types of optimization methods*

The choice of the method to use to solve a combinatorial optimization problem may depend on its complexity. In the case of problems of the class $\mathcal{P}$ a polynomial optimization algorithm can be used to solve the problem optimally.

In the case of problems of the class $\mathcal{NP}$ no polynomial optimization algorithm is found, and two approaches are possible (see Figure 2.1).

If the size of the problem is small, an exact algorithm can find the optimal solution (for example, branch-and-bound or dynamic programming). Unfortunately, these algorithms are based on enumerative procedures and may not be used on large size problems (although, in fact, the size is not the only limiting criterion). In the last case, it is recommended to use heuristic methods to find good solutions in a reasonable time, even if the optimality is not guaranteed. Among these methods there are either specific heuristic methods developed for a dedicated problem or metaheuristics that offer generic resolution schemes that can potentially be adapted to any type of optimization problem. Indeed, a metaheuristic may be defined as an algorithm designed to approximately solve a wide range of hard optimization problems without being deeply adapted to each problem [BOU 13].

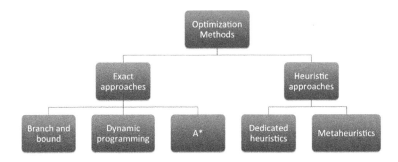

Figure 2.1. *Solving a problem from the class $\mathcal{NP}$*

The aim of such a metaheuristic is to explore the search space efficiently, without enumerating all the solutions. Then, a metaheuristic will be successful on a given optimization problem if it can provide a balance between the exploration (diversification) and the exploitation (intensification). Exploration is needed to identify regions of the search space with high quality solutions. Exploitation is important to intensify the search in those promising regions. The main differences between the existing metaheuristics concern the particular way in which they try to achieve this balance.

Hence modeling is an important phase in the analysis of a problem as problems of class $\mathcal{P}$ or $\mathcal{NP}$ cannot be tackled in exactly the same way. Moreover, the definition of the objective function is crucial but may be difficult to realize, especially for real-world problems.

2.2. Common concepts of metaheuristics

This section presents basic concepts that are common to any kind of metaheuristics. These concepts are linked to the three points listed above that are required to solve a combinatorial optimization problem. A more detailed presentation of these concepts may be found in [TAL 09].

2.2.1. *Representation/encoding*

Metaheuristics are generic methods to explore the search space of candidate (feasible or infeasible) solutions. Hence the design of a metaheuristic requires an encoding of these solutions. This is a key point, as the encoding plays an important role in the efficiency of the method. Indeed, for a given problem, several encodings may be used. Each encoding may be manipulated differently by the metaheuristic through optimization mechanisms (operators, evaluation function, etc.) that may be more or less efficient for the problem under study.

Some properties should be verified by the chosen encoding. First, any solution of the search space has to be encoded. Ideally, a single encoding must correspond to one candidate solution, but this is not always possible. Then, to be used by a metaheuristic, the encoding must respect the connexity property, which ensures that a search path exists between any two solutions, particularly with the optimum solution.

Regarding data mining problems, many encodings have been proposed. Among the most famous ones, we may cite:

– *Binary encoding:* the solution is represented by a vector of n binary values, representing decision variables of the problem. The search space is of size 2^n.

– *Vector of discrete values:* variables are not limited to binary values, but they may take discrete values.

– *Vector of real values:* variables can have real values.

– *Permutation:* the solution is described by a permutation of size n. With this representation, the size of the search space is of the order of $(n - 1)!$.

– *Graph based:* more sophisticated representations based on graphs and, in particular, on trees.

In addition, some indirect encodings may be proposed. In this case, a *decoder* is required to express the solution described by the encoding.

Finally, it is important to recall that the effectiveness of any encoding is strongly related to the mechanisms that will be applied to that specific encoding.

2.2.2. *Constraint satisfaction*

Optimization problems and, in particular, combinatorial ones are defined on a set of constraints to respect. Only candidate solutions that respect all these constraints are feasible. However, constraints may be difficult to respect and several strategies may be used to handle them:

– *Consider only feasible solutions:* any solution that does not satisfy a constraint will be discarded during the search.

– *Penalize infeasible solutions:* with this strategy, solutions that do not respect constraints are considered, but a penalization is applied to take unsatisfied constraints into account. Indeed, considering infeasible solutions may enable us to move to other regions of the search space and then favor diversification. This penalization may define a violation cost for every constraint and integrate it to the fitness function in a linear manner, for example. Another way to penalize infeasible solutions is to count the number of violated constraints or to evaluate the amount of infeasibility, which represents how far the solution is from a feasible solution.

– *Repair infeasible solutions:* this strategy consists of transforming an infeasible solution into a feasible one. This may be useful when operators generate frequently infeasible solutions.

The ultimate goal of optimization methods and, in particular, metaheuristics is to find the feasible solution that optimizes a given criterion (the objective function). Hence, depending on the facility of finding feasible solutions, one or the other strategies will provide better results.

2.2.3. *Optimization criterion/objective function*

The determination of the optimization criterion – which measures the quality of solutions – is crucial as the performance of the optimization process depends on it. Indeed, developing an efficient method that does not use the right criterion will lead us to obtain *the right answer to the wrong question*! One of the most difficult phases in turning a knowledge discovery task into an optimization problem is to define this optimization criterion that can be either specific to the data mining task or dependent on the application.

Once the optimization criterion is defined, the objective function f that represents the goal to achieve for the optimization method has to be formulated. Ideally, this objective function associates a real value with each solution of the search space, allowing a complete ordering of solutions of the search space:

$$f : \mathcal{D} \rightarrow \mathbf{R}$$

The objective function has to be defined very carefully, because it is useless to develop an efficient optimization method if the objective function is not properly defined. This objective function guides the search during the execution.

Then, regarding the optimization criterion (or the several criteria) that has been expressed for the problem under study, the objective function may translate it directly or may modify it in order to help the metaheuristic. This can happen when values of the optimization criterion are not enough different from a solution to another, for example.

Let us remark that it is often difficult to identify a single optimization criterion, especially for knowledge discovery problems, as most of the time, the *accuracy* of the solutions is as important as its *utility*, for example. Hence many real knowledge discovery problems are multi-objective by nature, because several optimization criteria have to be simultaneously considered.

Therefore, the use of optimization methods, in particular metaheuristics, requires particular attention on the way to define optimization criteria to deal with knowledge discovery problems. In the following chapters, dedicated to the different knowledge discovery tasks, this point is widely discussed.

2.2.4. *Performance analysis*

Metaheuristics are stochastic methods and performance analysis of such methods should be considered carefully. Particular attention should be paid to the comparison of several metaheuristics, to do it in a fair manner. This comparison may be useful to measure the contribution of a new search component, for example.

The first step of performance analysis deals with the *experimental design* that must specify the goals of the experiments (do we compare methods regarding quality of solutions, computational time, robustness, etc.?) and the benchmarks used (real benchmarks, random benchmarks, academic benchmarks constructed to *a priori* know the optimal solution, etc.).

Then, the *performance measures* and indicators must be identified to compute. They are linked directly to the goal of the experiments. To evaluate the quality of solutions, several indicators may be used depending on whether the optimal solution is known or not. If the optimal solution is known, then the difference in quality between the solution obtained and the known optimal solution can be computed. If the optimal solution is not known, then some lower/upper bounds may be used for computation. Otherwise, only comparative indicators between values obtained by the different methods may be used. Let us remark that the values compared are not systematically the values of the objective function, but may be the values of the optimization criterion identified for the problem.

To evaluate the computational time, the indicator may be, for example, the time needed to reach the optimal solution (if known and achievable) or to reach a given quality level. The difficulty with this measure is that the computational time depends on the computer architecture and results from the literature are difficult to compare.

With regard to robustness, an interesting point, for stochastic approaches, may be to measure the variability of quality of solutions produced by the same method among several runs. Moreover, it can be interesting to evaluate the impact of small deviations on the instance description on the quality of solutions.

Given all the performance measures that are computable, most of the time for several runs, on several problem instances (or datasets), a statistical analysis must be used to conduct the performance assessment of metaheuristics. Therefore, statistical tests are performed to estimate whether the confidence of the results is valid.

An additional difficulty to evaluate the performance of metaheuristics when dealing with data mining problems is in measuring the interest of the solution, that is to say the extracted knowledge, when applied to new data. Chapter 1 provided some indications on this point, but it can be interesting to differentiate two points of view for performance analysis:

– *Optimization point of view:* the aim of the performance analysis is to evaluate the ability of the method to explore the search space and find a solution of good quality (most of the time in comparison with other methods).

– *Data mining point of view:* the aim of the performance analysis is to evaluate the interest of the knowledge extracted and, in particular, its ability to deal with unknown data.

2.3. Single solution-based/local search methods

Among metaheuristics, many works make the difference between single solution-based and population-based metaheuristics [TAL 09, BOU 13]. The first ones work on a single solution, improving it iteratively such as a walk in the search space. Metaheuristics from the second type work on a set of solutions, combining them to extract good properties of solutions. In our view, the main difference between the two types is the opposition between local improvements in the first type and global improvements in the second type. Moreover, in the context of multi-objective optimization, some metaheuristics from the first type have been adapted to this context, working with an archive of solutions, but still keeping the local aspect of the method. Thus, we divide metaheuristics into two categories:

– *local search methods*, instead of single solution-based methods;

– *population-based methods.*

Several local search metaheuristics and their extensions have been proposed. The main common concept for these methods is the application on the current solution of a local transformation, called a neighborhood operator. Thus, this concept is defined in this section and then several well-known local search methods are presented.

2.3.1. *Neighborhood of a solution*

With any feasible solution s, it is possible to associate a set of neighbors, generated from s using a local transformation. The aim of this transformation is to modify the solution locally and not to change its global structure *a priori*, leading to the creation of a neighboring solution. Hence the main properties of s should be kept. This neighborhood operator should be carefully defined regarding the problem under study and the representation of solution used.

DEFINITION 2.1.– *The neighborhood of* s, *denoted by* $\mathcal{N}(s)$, *is the set of solutions that may be obtained from* s *using a local transformation called the neighborhood operator* $\mathcal{N}$.

$$\mathcal{N} : s \to \mathcal{N}(s)$$

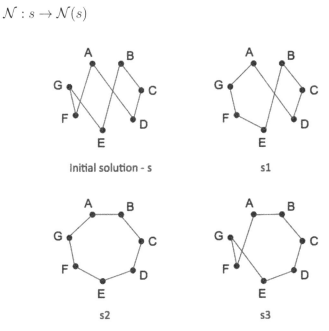

Figure 2.2. *Neighborhood operator for the TSP*

To illustrate this neighborhood notion, let us consider a traveling salesman problem with seven towns to be visited exactly once (A, B, C, D, E, F and G). Solutions may be encoded with the ordered list of towns visited. Several neighborhood operators may be defined (see Figure 2.2):

– *move:* move the position of one town;

– *exchange:* exchange the position of two towns;

– *inverse:* inverse a sub-sequence of towns.

Given s an initial solution: A D C B E G F:

   – by moving F, we may obtain $s1$: A D C B E F G;

   – by exchanging A and E, we may obtain $s2$: E D C B A G F;

   – by inversing the sub-sequence D C B, we may obtain $s3$: A B C D E G F.

As illustrated, at least three operators may be defined for this problem. The neighborhood structure defined, thanks to the operator, plays a crucial role in the performance of metaheuristics and may lead to efficient, or inefficient, optimization methods. Hence the design of the neighborhood operator should be carried out with care.

In addition to this neighborhood definition, the concept of local optimum must be defined.

DEFINITION 2.2.– *Given a neighborhood operator $\mathcal{N}$, a solution $s \in \mathcal{D}$ is a local optimum if none of its neighbors has a better quality. In a minimization context, this may be expressed by: s is a local optimum, iff $\forall s' \in \mathcal{N}(s)$, $f(s) \leq f(s')$.*

Based on the neighborhood operator, several local search paradigms have been proposed. Their main difficulty is to escape from the local optima, as, by definition, an application of the neighborhood operator on a local optimum solution cannot improve its quality. The rest of this section is dedicated to the presentation of well-known local search methods and reveals the mechanisms they use to escape from the local optima.

2.3.2. *Hill climbing algorithm*

The hill climbing algorithm (HC) is the simplest metaheuristic. It starts with an initial solution, explores its neighborhood and selects the next current solution. Hence given a neighborhood operator $\mathcal{N}$ may be described by algorithm 2.1, for a minimization problem.

This algorithm stops either when a stopping criterion is reached (for example, a limit number of iterations, a limit amount of time, etc.), or usually when no improving neighbors may be found. In this case, a local optimum is found and the last current solution s is then the best solution encountered during the search. Several implementations of this simple algorithm may be realized, regarding the way the neighbor s' is selected. Several *selection* strategies may be considered:

– *Best improvement:* in this strategy, the best neighbor is selected among the whole neighborhood. This requires to generate and evaluate all the neighbors of the current solution exhaustively (exhaustive exploration of the neighborhood).

– *First improvement:* in this strategy, the first improving neighbor encountered is selected. This may avoid the exploration of the whole neighborhood. To introduce diversity within the neighborhood exploration, it is preferred to generate neighbors in a random manner.

– *Other strategies:* for example, in the random improvement, several neighbors are generated and a random selection is made among the improving ones.

Algorithm 2.1. Simple hill climbing algorithm

Given $s \in \mathcal{D}$
while Stopping criterion not met **do**
  Select $s' \in \mathcal{N}(s)$
  if $f(s') < f(s)$ **then**
    $s \leftarrow s'$
  end if
end while

The main drawback of the HC algorithm is that it stops as soon as a local optimum is encountered. Some mechanisms have been proposed to escape from the local optimum. They lead to the proposition of other local search methods, such as Tabu Search (TS), simulated annealing and others.

2.3.3. *Tabu Search*

TS was initially proposed by Glover [GLO 89]. The principle is to accept, in some cases, non-improving neighbors to escape from the local optima. This method first works like the HC algorithm. However, when a local optimum is reached, the method accepts a non-improving neighbor (in general, the best solution of the neighborhood) as the next current solution. Let us remark that in this case, the current solution at the end of the search may not be the best encountered during the search and that it is required to memorize s^* as the best solution. After selecting a non-improving neighbor as the current solution, the next move may create a cycle between this neighbor and the local optimum. To avoid such cycles, TS forbids to return to solutions that have been recently visited using a memory. This memory, called Tabu list, may store either the last visited solutions or the last visited moves. In this last case, a Tabu move can still be applied if it enables us to reach a better solution than s^*. This mechanism is managed by the aspiration criterion. The design of the method must specify the management of the Tabu list.

In a minimization context, the Tabu Search algorithm may be described in Algorithm 2.2.

Algorithm 2.2. Tabu Search

Given $s \in \mathcal{D}$

$s^* \leftarrow s$ /*initialization of the best solution*/

$T \leftarrow \emptyset$ /*initialization of the tabu list*/

while Stopping criterion not met **do**

    Select the best neighbor $s' \in \mathcal{N}(s)$, $s' \notin T$

    $s \leftarrow s'$

    Update T

    if $f(s) < f(s^*)$ **then**

        $s^* \leftarrow s$

    end if

end while

2.3.4. *Simulated annealing and threshold acceptance approach*

Simulated annealing (SA) method was proposed by physicians Kirkpatrick, Gelatt and Vecchi in 1983 [KIR 83]. This method is inspired from the annealing technique used by metallurgists to obtain a "well-organized" material that consists of heating a material and making its temperature to decrease slowly to allow atoms having a good organization that would correspond to an optimum. The SA process uses a parameter T, called $Temperature$, that decreases all along the search. Depending on the value of this parameter, the probability of accepting a non-improving neighbor is set. Hence SA starts by generating an initial solution, then a neighbor is generated and the probability of acceptance is computed with its quality and the value of the parameter T. The algorithm may be described in Algorithm 2.3.

Algorithm 2.3. Simulated annealing

Given $s \in \mathcal{D}$

$s^* \leftarrow s$ /*initialization of the best solution*/

Initialize T /*initialization of the temperature parameter*/

while Not stopping criterion **do**

　Select a neighbor $s' \in \mathcal{N}(s)$

　if $f(s') < f(s)$ **then**

　　$s \leftarrow s'$

　else

　　$s \leftarrow s'$ with a probability $p(T, f(s'), f(s))$

　end if

　if $f(s) < f(s^*)$ **then**

　　$s^* \leftarrow s$ /*Update the best solution*/

　end if

　Update T /*Decrease T if necessary */

end while

Deriving from this method, the *threshold acceptance* (TA) method has been proposed [DUE 90]. The main difference is that instead of using a temperature parameter to guide acceptance of a non-improving neighbor, as in SA, the TA approach computes the degradation of the objective function induced by the new neighbor and accepts it if it does not exceed a decreasing threshold T, as described in Algorithm 2.4.

2.3.5. *Combining local search approaches*

Local search methods are efficient to improve the quality of a solution quickly. The main drawback is their difficulty in exploring the whole search space leading to local optima solutions whose quality is not always satisfactory. Hence several approaches have been proposed to improve the quality of solutions produced by local search methods. Among them, we may cite:

– *Iterated local search (ILS):* an ILS consists of executing the same local search method in sequence, such that the initial solution of the next iteration is obtained by applying a perturbation on a previously visited solution. This perturbation mechanism favors the exploration, by the local search method, of other parts of the search space [LOU 10].

– *Variable neighborhood search (VNS):* this local search uses several neighborhood operators to improve the search space exploration. It iteratively selects one neighborhood operator and executes a local search using this operator. The choice of the operator is based on a predefined neighborhood structure that should select complementary neighborhood operators [MLA 97].

– *Guided local search (GLS):* another way to modify the structure of the search space is not to modify the neighborhood operator, but to modify the objective function. This is the strategy of GLS that dynamically changes the objective function to escape from the local optima [VOU 99].

– *Greedy randomized adaptive search procedure (GRASP):* the GRASP method consists of executing two phases iteratively: the first one constructs a feasible solution using a randomized greedy heuristic while the second one applies a local search on this initial solution [FEO 95].

Algorithm 2.4. Threshold acceptance

Given $s \in \mathcal{D}$
$s^* \leftarrow s$ /*initialization of the best solution*/
Initialize T /*initialization of the threshold*/
while Stopping criterion not met **do**
  Select a neighbor $s' \in \mathcal{N}(s)$
  if $f(s') - f(s) < T$ **then**
    $s \leftarrow s'$
  end if
  if $f(s) < f(s^*)$ **then**
    $s^* \leftarrow s$ /*Update the best solution*/
  end if
  Update T /*Decrease T if necessary */
end while

Many strategies have been proposed to exploit the efficiency of local search approaches. Moreover, although these methods are metaheuristics and then should be generic approaches, some of them exploit the structure of the problem under study, leading to numerous different optimization methods. Another type of metaheuristics are population-based metaheuristics that deal with a set of solutions instead of a single solution and its neighborhood.

2.4. Population-based metaheuristics

As they manipulate a set of solutions, population-based metaheuristics offer a good opportunity to explore the search space. Most of these approaches are based on analogies with natural concepts. Hence evolutionary computation algorithms are inspired by Darwin's evolutionary theory and the nature's capability to evolve living beings well-adapted to their environment. This is the subject of the first part of this section. In the second part, algorithms inspired from swarm intelligence are presented.

2.4.1. *Evolutionary computation*

Evolutionary computation (EC) groups several metaheuristics that have a similar structure in common [YAO 05, TAL 09, BOU 13]. A population of candidate solutions, called individuals, is created and each individual is evaluated. Then, processes of selection, recombination and mutation are applied, creating a generation, leading to a new population of better quality. Algorithm 2.5 describes the general scheme of EC approaches.

Algorithm 2.5. General evolutionary computation approaches

Initialize *population* $\mathcal{P}_i$ of individuals
while Stopping criterion not met **do**
   Select *parents* from $\mathcal{P}_i$
   Apply search operators (recombination, mutation)
   Evaluate new individuals
   Construct the next *population* $\mathcal{P}_{i+1}$
end while

Most famous and used algorithms from EC are genetic algorithms (GA), evolution strategy (ES), evolutionary programming (EP) and genetic programming (GP).

2.4.1.1. *Genetic algorithm*

Genetic algorithms (GAs) were developed initially by Holland [HOL 75, GOL 88] and are the most widely used evolutionary computation technique. Designing such an algorithm requires defining the representation of solutions (called *chromosomes*), the selection strategy, the search operators (*crossover* and *mutation*), etc. The aim of the selection strategy is to choose individuals (called *parents*) that will be used for the construction of the next generation. This is mostly based on the fitness values of solutions that represent their ability to answer the problem to solve. One of the specificities of GAs is the crossover operator that combines several individuals (the parents) and exchanges parts of them to create one or several *offsprings*. The objective is to share good characteristics to obtain better quality *offsprings*. Since in the first GAs, chromosomes were mostly encoded by fixed length binary strings, many classical crossover operators adapted to this representation have been proposed, such as 1-point crossover (or more generally n-point crossover), uniform crossover, etc.

Nowadays, development of GAs is not limited to bit string encodings, but other representations have been proposed to deal with various types of optimization problems. This will be the case for knowledge discovery problems, as will be discussed later in this book.

2.4.1.2. *Evolution strategy*

ES is another way to copy the principles of natural evolution that was proposed originally by Rechenberg [REC 65, REC 73]. First ES were dedicated to parameter optimization and applied mostly to continuous optimization. Hence representations are based on real-values vectors. Such methods are based on an elitist replacement, a normally (Gaussian) distributed mutation and rarely on a crossover to evolve a population of μ parents to create $\lambda > \mu$ *offsprings*. Hence considering parents or not to form the next population, will lead to two different strategies ($(\mu + \lambda)$-ES or (μ, λ)-ES). Extension of these strategies are $(\mu/\rho + \lambda)$-ES and $(\mu/\rho, \lambda)$-ES, where $/\rho$ indicates the number of parents involved in the creation of offsprings. One of the interests of these methods is the large theory on convergence that has been developed [BEY 13].

2.4.1.3. *Evolutionary programming*

EP, initially proposed by Fogel *et al.* [FOG 66], uses mutation operators exclusively to generate *offsprings*. No recombination is applied and the *parent* selection mechanism is deterministic. Mutation operators consist of adding to the parents a random number of a certain distribution. Several of them have been proposed by different authors. EP is very similar to ES and, therefore, is not widely used.

2.4.1.4. *Genetic programming*

GP groups more recent approaches. They were proposed by Koza in the early 1990s [KOZ 92]. GPs are very similar to GAs, but the main difference is that individuals are themselves programs. A tree representation is used. Leaves of the tree (called *terminals* in GP) represent variables and constants and internal nodes represent arithmetic operations (called *functions*). As in GAs, parent selection is mostly fitness proportional and a generational replacement is adopted. Specific operators managing trees are required. Crossover operators may be based on tree (or sub-tree) exchanges and mutation operators may be based on random changes in the tree. The reader may refer to [SHA 06] for examples of such operators. One of the difficulties in GP is the variable length representation, as programs encoded may be of several sizes. GPs are widely used in machine learning and data mining tasks.

2.4.1.5. *Other evolutionary computation approaches*

Other EC approaches have been proposed in the literature and some of them are cited below:

– *Estimation of distribution algorithms (EDA):* also known as probabilistic model-building genetic algorithms (PMBGA) or iterated density estimation evolutionary algorithms (IDEA), EDAs encode the knowledge accumulated during the search in well-structured models [SHA 06]. These models are learnt from good individuals (probabilistic estimation of promising solutions) and used to create new individuals. This should lead the search towards promising areas of the search space. EDAs have been applied with success on a variety of problems; however, many questions are still open regarding their behavior.

– *Differential evolution (DE):* applied with success to solve continuous optimization problems, DE approaches are recently proposed evolutionary algorithms [STO 97]. Each individual is encoded by a vector of real values. The specificities of these approaches are the operators. The crossover operator does not combine part of parents' chromosome as in classical EAs, but makes a linear combination of three randomly chosen solutions. Similarly, the mutation operator computes vector differences with other randomly chosen solutions to generate the mutated solution. DE is a simple method that has the advantage of requiring only a few control parameters and is then easy to tune.

– *Co-evolutionary algorithms:* based on the observation of coevolution of species in nature, co-evolutionary algorithms involve several populations, each one representing a species [HIL 90]. One of the specificities in co-evolutionary algorithms is that the individual fitness is not an absolute fitness as in most approaches, but is a subjective value. Indeed, the fitness of an individual in a population will depend on the fitness of individuals of the other populations. In a competitive model, the different populations compete to solve the problem, whereas in a cooperative model, the different populations cooperate to improve their survival.

– *Scatter search (SS):* originally presented by F. Glover [GLO 77], SS is an evolutionary metaheuristic that combines solutions from a reference set (which contains diversified feasible solutions of good quality) to create new ones. These new solutions may be infeasible and are, therefore, repaired. They are then improved using a local search, for example. Obtained solutions are used to update the reference set and the population, if necessary. Principles of SS may be found in [MAR 06], but it is interesting to note that SS integrates components from local search approaches as well as evolutionary algorithms. In addition, *path relinking (PR)* has been proposed with SS to connect good solutions produced by SS [GLO 98]. Indeed, the aim of PR is to generate and explore the trajectory between a starting solution and a target solution. These two solutions can be local optima found by SS, and the objective is to explore intermediate solutions (possibly infeasible ones) that may lead to good quality feasible solutions.

2.4.2. *Swarm intelligence*

Swarm intelligence (SI) refers to algorithms or distributed problem-solving devices inspired by the collective behavior of social insect colonies (such as ants, bees, wasps, etc.) and other animal societies (such as fishes, birds, etc.) [BON 99]. The main principle of such algorithms is to work with a set of simple particles that is able to interact with other particles and with their environment. Those interactions may lead to the emergence of a global and self-organized behavior. Interested readers may refer to the book of Engelbrecht to obtain information about the mathematical models of social collective behaviors [ENG 06]. Moreover, other books have been proposed on these types of approaches and their applications (in bioinformatics, for example; the reader may refer to [DAS 08]).

Ant colony optimization algorithms and particle swarm optimization are the two most famous algorithms in this category. They are presented shortly hereafter. However, many other approaches based on different analogies have been proposed: the bee colony optimization approach [KAR 09], the bacterial foraging optimization algorithm [PAS 02], the artificial immune systems [TIM 10] and others.

2.4.2.1. *Ant colony optimization algorithms*

Ant colony optimization algorithms (ACO) were proposed by M. Dorigo in the 1990s [DOR 92]. In ACOs, a population of artificial ants cooperates with each other to find the best path in a graph, representing a candidate solution to the target problem, analogously to the way that natural ants cooperate to find the shortest path between two points such as between their nest and a food source. Indeed, while walking from food sources to the nest and vice versa, natural ants deposit an odorous and volatile substance, called *pheromone*, on the ground. When an ant decides the direction to take, it chooses with higher probability the path that is marked by stronger pheromone concentrations, which leads to the emergence of shortest paths.

Artificial ant colonies simulate this behavior to construct solutions for an optimization problem. Therefore, the problem under study is modeled as a completely connected graph, whose nodes are components of solutions. A solution to the problem is encoded as a feasible walk in this graph. A pheromone value (pheromone trail) is associated with each solution's component and guides the construction of the solution. The interested reader can refer to the survey presented by Dorigo *et al.* [DOR 05]. A global overview is presented in Algorithm 2.6.

Such algorithms have been traditionally applied to the traveling salesman problem (TSP), but also used successfully for classification problems, for example, leading to the proposition of *cAnt-Miner algorithm* to discover a set of classification rules [OTE 08]. Improvements are still currently proposed to address other types of data [OTE 15].

Algorithm 2.6. General ant colony optimization algorithm

Initialize pheromone values
while Stopping criterion not met **do**
  for all ants **do**
    Construct solutions using the pheromone trail
    Update pheromone trails (evaporation, reinforcement)
  end for
end while

2.4.2.2. *Particle swarm optimization*

Particle swarm optimization (PSO) is a global optimization technique developed by Kennedy and Eberhart in 1995 [KEN 95]. This population-based stochastic algorithm for optimization is based on social–psychological principles. The original intent was to simulate the graceful but unpredictable choreography of a bird flock graphically. Unlike evolutionary algorithms, the particle swarm does not use selection; typically, all population members survive from the beginning of a trial until the end. Their interactions result in iterative improvement of the quality of problem solutions over time [EBE 01].

In PSO, autonomous particles (representing solutions) are generated randomly in the search space. With each particle is associated a velocity, a location in the search space and a memory to keep track of the best solution it has achieved so far (the personal best solution of particle i, $pbest_i$). Another best value, the global best, $gbest$, is also memorized. The particle swarm optimization concept consists, at each time step, of changing the velocity (accelerating) of each particle toward its $pbest$ and $gbest$ locations taking into account the social influence between particles. A general scheme of the algorithm is given in Algorithm 2.7. For more details about computation (velocities, locations, etc.), readers may refer to [KEN 10].

2.5. Multi-objective metaheuristics

As mentioned earlier, metaheuristics are very powerful tools for solving complex single-objective optimization problems. However, many real-world problems have two or more optimization criteria (which may represent several objective functions), often conflicting with each other, that need to be optimized at the same time. This is also the case in data mining, where the objective function may often be a balance between accuracy of the model extracted and its simplicity, for example. These problems are called *multi-objective*. Their resolution involves finding several – not only one – solutions that represent the best possible compromises (or trade-offs) among all the objectives that are to be optimized. Regarding the data mining context, A. Freitas presents a position paper that makes a critical review of multi-objective optimization in data mining. This paper compares several approaches and concludes on their interest for data mining problems [FRE 04]. In this section, we will first give some basic definitions about multi-objective optimization and then present some classical metaheuristics dedicated to solve these problems.

Algorithm 2.7. Particle swarm optimization algorithm

Initialize randomly particles
while Stopping criterion not met **do**
    for all particles i **do**
        Update velocity
        Move to new position x_i
    end for
    if $f(x_i) < f(pbest_i)$ **then**
        $pbest_i \leftarrow x_i$
        if $f(x_i) < f(gbest)$ **then**
            $gbest \leftarrow x_i$
        end if
    end if
end while

2.5.1. *Basic notions in multi-objective optimization*

This section presents the main concepts about multi-objective optimization. For more detailed information, readers can refer to [COE 10b].

2.5.1.1. *Definitions*

A multi-objective optimization problem is defined by a set of solutions $\mathcal{D}$ – the decision space – and a set of n ($n \geq 2$) objective functions f_i that associate with each solution s n values (usually real values) that represent its quality regarding several criteria. Such a problem is described by:

$$optimize\ F(s) = (f_1(s), f_2(s), ..., f_n(s))$$

$$s \in \mathcal{D}$$

where objective function f_i has to be optimized (maximized or minimized). Solutions of the decision are of different natures and are defined by constraints that determine feasible solutions. In the case of a finite set of discrete solutions $\mathcal{D}$, the problem becomes a multi-objective combinatorial optimization problem ($MOCOP$).

Unlike single-objective optimization, the solution of a $MOCOP$ is not unique, but is composed of a set of solutions representing the best possible trade-offs (or compromises) among the objectives. Thus, this leads to a different notion of optimality from that in single-objective optimization. The notion of optimality that is most commonly adopted was originally proposed by Francis Ysidro Edgeworth in 1881 [EDG 81] and later generalized by Vilfredo Pareto in 1896 [PAR 96]. Although some authors call this notion the Edgeworth–Pareto optimality, the most commonly accepted term is Pareto optimality.

A feasible solution $s^* \in \mathcal{D}$ is called *Pareto optimal* (also called efficient or non-dominated) if and only if there is no solution $s \in \mathcal{D}$, such that s dominates s^*, where a solution s_1 dominates a solution s_2, in a minimization context if and only if $\forall i \in [1...n], f_i(s_1) \leq f_i(s_2)$ and $\exists i \in [1...n]$, such that $f_i(s_1) < f_i(s_2)$.

In this context, any solution of the *Pareto optimal set* (composed of Pareto optimal solutions) may be considered as optimal, since no improvement may be found on all the objective functions simultaneously. Hence an improvement for one objective value induces a degradation on another objective value. When plotting the objective function values corresponding to the solutions stored in the Pareto optimal set in the objective space, the *Pareto front* of the problem is obtained.

Figure 2.3 illustrates in the objective space, for a bi-objective minimization problem, the Pareto dominance property and indicates the ideal point that represents for the two objectives the best values, but is unfeasible.

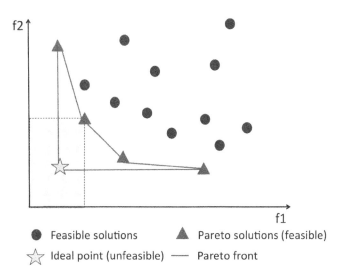

Figure 2.3. *Objective space and specific*
points of a bi-objective problem

2.5.1.2. *Dealing with a multi-objective optimization problem*

The first studies of multi-objective optimization problems transformed them into a succession of single-objective optimization problems. This involved the use of approaches such as lexicographic ordering – which optimizes one objective at a time, considering first the most important one, as defined by the user – and linear aggregating functions – which use a weighted sum of the objectives, where weights indicate the importance of each of them, as defined by the user. Over the years, other types of approaches have been proposed, aiming to provide compromise solutions without the need of incorporating explicit preferences from the user. Today, many multi-objective metaheuristics incorporate mechanisms to select and store solutions that represent the best possible compromises among all the objectives, without any need to rank or to add all the objectives. In this case, solving a multi-objective optimization problem involves two phases:

– *Search for the best possible compromises:* in this stage, any search algorithm can be adopted and normally no preference information is adopted. The aim is to produce as many compromise solutions as possible and to have them as spread out as possible, such that a wide range of possible compromises can be obtained.

– *Selection of a single solution:* once the number of compromise solutions have been computed, the decision maker has to select one for the task at hand. This phase involves a process called multi-criteria decision-making.

Usually, these two phases are considered in sequence, except in interactive approaches, where the decision maker is involved in the search of the compromises. Hence even if this second phase is very challenging and leads to important question, it is not directly linked to the optimization process and we focus on the first phase: the search of the Pareto optimal set.

2.5.2. *Multi-objective optimization using metaheuristics*

Most $MOCOPs$ are NP-hard and even if some exact methods have been proposed to solve multi-objective optimization problems (for example [DHA 10]), they can be used only for small-scale problems. Thus, the use of metaheuristics in this field has become increasingly popular [DEB 01, COE 07, COE 10a]. This part first proposes a classification of metaheuristics for multi-objective optimization and then presents some well-known ones, as shown in [COE 10b].

2.5.2.1. *Classification of multi-objective metaheuristics*

Multi-objective metaheuristics can be classified into four classes:

– *Scalar approaches:* they transform the problem into one or several single-objective problem(s). Among them, there are aggregation methods [ISH 98], ϵ-constraint method [HER 94], weighted metrics, goal programming, achievement functions, goal attainment, etc. These methods require *a priori* knowledge of the problem to define preferences among objectives and usually they produce a single solution per run.

– *Population-based approaches:* they exploit the population adopted by several metaheuristics (for example, evolutionary algorithms) to combine several scalar search procedures in a single run. The typical example within this group is the vector evaluated genetic algorithm proposed by Schaffer [SCH 85], which consists of a simple genetic algorithm that uses as many sub-populations as the number of objectives of the problem. Each sub-population selects the best individuals based on a single objective. Then, all the sub-populations are merged and shuffled, and crossover and mutation operators are applied as usual. The idea is based on the principle that recombining individuals that are good in one objective function may generate good compromise solutions. Such kinds of approaches, however, contradict the notion of Pareto optimality and is rarely used these days.

– *Pareto-based approaches:*   in this case, the selection mechanism incorporates the concept of Pareto optimality. Typical approaches within this class adopt a ranking of solutions based on Pareto optimality originally proposed by D.E. Goldberg [GOL 89]. Indeed, many multi-objective evolutionary algorithms are based on Pareto ranking, although several variations are available: dominance rank (MOGA [FON 93]), dominance depth (NSGA-II [DEB 02]), dominance count (SPEA[ZIT 99b] and SPEA2 [ZIT 01]).

– *Indicator-based approaches:*   in this case, instead of using the Pareto ranking, a performance assessment measure [ZIT 03] is adopted to select solutions. Typical methods within this class are the indicator-based evolutionary algorithm (IBEA) [ZIT 04, BAS 06] and the S-metric selection EMOA (SMS-EMOA) [BEU 07]).

The following section is dedicated to the presentation of the most widely used multi-objective metaheuristics and, in particular, Pareto-based and indicator-based ones. A paragraph is also dedicated to the presentation of multi-objective local search approaches.

2.5.2.2. *Non-dominated sorting genetic algorithm II (NSGA-II)*

The non-dominated sorting genetic algorithm II was proposed by Deb *et al.* [DEB 02] and is probably the most commonly used multi-objective evolutionary algorithm in the current literature. At each generation, solutions from the current population are ranked into several classes. Individuals mapping to vectors from the first front all belong to the best efficient set; individuals mapping to vectors from the second front all belong to the second best efficient set and so on. Two values are then assigned to population members. The first one corresponds to the rank the corresponding solution belongs to and represents the quality of the solution in terms of convergence. The second one, called crowding distance, consists of estimating the density of solutions surrounding a particular point of the objective space, and represents the quality of the solution in terms of diversity. A solution is said to be better than another if it has a better rank value, or, in case of equality, if it has a better crowding distance. The selection strategy is a deterministic tournament between two randomly selected solutions. At the replacement step, only the best individuals survive with respect to a predefined population size.

2.5.2.3. *Strength Pareto evolutionary algorithm 2 (SPEA2)*

The strength Pareto evolutionary algorithm 2 [ZIT 01] was proposed as an extension of the strength Pareto evolutionary algorithm (SPEA) [ZIT 99b], introduced by the same authors. The main improvements are related to the use of an improved fitness assignment strategy. SPEA2 handles an internal archive of fixed size that is used during the selection step to create offspring solutions. Also, an external archive that stores the non-dominated solutions generated during the search is adopted. At a given iteration of SPEA2, to each population and archive member s is assigned a strength value $S(s)$ representing the number of solutions it dominates. Then, the fitness value $F(s)$ of solution s is calculated by summing up the strength values of all individuals that solution s currently dominates. Additionally, a diversity preservation strategy, based on a nearest-neighbor technique, is incorporated. The selection step consists of a binary tournament with replacement applied on the internal archive only.

2.5.2.4. *Indicator-based evolutionary algorithm (IBEA)*

The IBEA was introduced in [ZIT 04] and is a framework that allows any performance indicator to be incorporated into the selection mechanism of a multi-objective evolutionary algorithm. The main idea behind IBEA is to introduce a total order among solutions by means of a binary quality indicator. Its fitness assignment scheme is based on a pairwise comparison of solutions from the current population with regard to an arbitrary indicator I. To each individual s is assigned a fitness value $F(s)$ measuring the *loss in quality* if s was removed from the current population. Different indicators can be used for such a purpose, such as the binary additive ϵ-indicator ($I_\epsilon+$), as defined in [ZIT 04], or the hypervolume difference [ZIT 99a]. Selection for reproduction consists of a binary tournament between randomly chosen individuals. Selection for replacement consists of iteratively removing the worst solution from the current population until the required population size is reached; fitness information of the remaining individuals is updated each time when there is a deletion.

2.5.2.5. *Simple elitist evolutionary algorithm (SEEA)*

If evaluating a solution in the objective space is not too much time consuming, computing fitness values and diversity information are generally the most computationally expensive steps of a multi-objective evolutionary algorithm. Based on this observation, Liefooghe *et al.* [LIE 08] proposed a simple search method for which none of these phases is required. In the resulting evolutionary algorithm, called the SEEA, an archive of potentially efficient solutions is updated at each generation, and the individuals contained in the main population are generated by applying variation operators to randomly chosen archive members. The replacement step is a generational one, i.e. the parent population is replaced by the offspring population. Note that the initial population can, for instance, be filled with random solutions. Then, the archive is not only used as an external storage, but it is integrated into the optimization process during the selection phase of the multi-objective evolutionary algorithm. The preservation of the non-dominated solutions generated during the search is called elitism and its use is of great importance in multi-objective optimization, since it is required to guarantee convergence from a theoretical point of view [RUD 00]. SEEA is somehow related to other elitist multi-objective evolutionary algorithms such as the Pareto envelope-based selection algorithm for multi-objective optimization (PESA) [COR 00] and the simple evolutionary algorithm for multi-objective optimization (SEAMO) [VAL 02]. However, contrary to other approaches, no strategy to preserve diversity or to manage the size of the archive is involved here, as solutions are selected randomly and the archive is unbounded.

2.5.2.6. *Multi-objective local search approaches (MOLS)*

As described earlier, evolutionary algorithms are also well-adapted to deal with multi-objective optimization, as they work with a population of solutions. However, some local search approaches have also been extended to the multi-objective context leading to the proposition of multi-objective local search approaches (MOLS). Some of them may be grouped within the term DMLS (dominance-based multi-objective local search) [LIE 12]. Those approaches use a dominance relation, like Pareto dominance, to handle each objective separately. Thus, the main difference with single-objective approaches is that they have to cope with a population of compromise solutions, instead of one single solution. Several algorithms have been proposed, like Pareto local search (PLS) [PAQ 04] or Pareto archived evolution strategy (PAES) [KNO 00].

2.5.2.7. *General components*

As presented above, the adaptation of metaheuristics to multi-objective optimization generally requires three main components:

– a mechanism to select solutions that are non-dominated in the Pareto sense;

– a mechanism to maintain diversity to promote convergence to the entire Pareto front;

– an elitist mechanism that ensures non-dominated solutions discovered during the search to be preserved throughout the search.

2.5.3. *Performance assessment in multi-objective optimization*

An important task while validating a multi-objective metaheuristic is to be able to assess its performance with respect to other approaches. This task should be done with care, since the two algorithms compared generate sets of solutions that are approximation of the true Pareto front, rather than a single value. Several performance indicators have been proposed to perform this task. These indicators depend on different features, such as unary versus binary definitions or requirement of the true Pareto front. Moreover, regarding the quality expected from the Pareto front, the performance assessment may deal with convergence evaluation, diversity evaluation or both. For more details on performance assessment of multi-objective metaheuristics, see [KNO 02, ZIT 03].

Performance indicators can be classified according to different features [COE 10b]:

– *Unary/binary indicators:* binary indicators allow us to compare two approximations of the true Pareto front directly, whereas unary indicators assign to each approximation a scalar value.

– *Requirement of the true Pareto front:* some performance indicators require that the user provides the true Pareto front of the problem, which, in many cases, is unknown.

– *Need of extra information:* some quality indicators require the definition of several values that may be difficult to obtain in some cases (for example, the ideal point, the nadir point, a reference solution set, etc.).

A lot of performance indicators are available currently; however, their use is not only standardized, but it is debatable in several cases. Usually, more than one performance indicator is adopted to assess the performance of a multi-objective metaheuristic. This is why different indicators exist for different goals:

– *Convergence-based indicators:* they provide the closeness of the obtained approximation with respect to the true Pareto front. Examples of this kind of indicators are: contribution [MEU 00], generational distance [VAN 00] and ϵ-indicator [ZIT 03].

– *Diversity-based indicators:* they provide information about the uniformity of the distribution of the obtained solutions along the Pareto front. Examples of this kind of indicators are: spacing [VAN 00], spread [DEB 01, DEB 02] and entropy [FAR 02].

– *Hybrid indicators:* they attempt to combine, in a single value, the performance on both convergence and diversity. Examples of this kind of indicators are: hypervolume [ZIT 99a] and the R-metrics [KNO 02].

2.6. Conclusion

Metaheuristics are generic methods that are able to deal with numerous optimization problems. Their diversity and their flexibility make this class of methods very attractive to tackle challenging problems that appear in data mining, particularly in the context of Big Data. This is the scope of the following chapters.

Metaheuristics and Parallel Optimization

The growth of data and the need for performance lead to the need for power. In computer science, to obtain power, it is common to use parallelism and parallel computation. Parallelism is often associated with Big Data. For metaheuristics, it is also very common as parallelized metaheuristics allow us not only to solve larger problems, but also to obtain more robust metaheuristics of parallel computing and then focus on parallel metaheuristics. A brief overview on infrastructure and technologies for parallel metaheuristics will then be provided. This chapter ends on the quality measures frequently used.

3.1. Parallelism

Parallel computing is a type of computation in which many calculations are carried out simultaneously, operating on the principle that large problems can often be divided into smaller ones, which are then solved at the same time [ALM 89]. There are several different forms of parallel computing: bit-level, instruction-level, data and task parallelism [WIK 16a]. The last two forms are the more common in parallel metaheuristics.

3.1.1. *Bit-level*

Bit-level parallelism is a form of parallel computing based on increasing processor word size. From the advent of very-large-scale integration (VLSI) computer chip fabrication technology in the 1970s until 1986, advancements in computer architecture were brought about by increasing bit-level parallelism [CUL 97].

3.1.2. *Instruction-level parallelism*

A computer program is, in essence, a stream of instructions executed by a processor. These instructions can be reordered and combined into groups that are then executed in parallel without changing the result of the program. This is known as instruction-level parallelism. Advances in instruction-level parallelism dominated computer architecture from the mid-1980s until the mid-1990s.

Modern processors have multi-stage instruction pipelines. Each stage in the pipeline corresponds to a different action the processor performs on that instruction in that stage; a processor with an N-stage pipeline can have up to N different instructions at different stages of completion.

3.1.3. *Task and data parallelism*

Task parallelisms is the characteristic of a parallel program where different calculations/tasks can be performed on the same or different sets of data [WIK 16b]. Task parallelism involves the decomposition of a task into sub-tasks and then allocating each sub-task to a processor for execution. The processors would then execute these sub-tasks simultaneously and often cooperatively. Task parallelism does not usually scale with the size of a problem.

Data parallelism focuses on distributing the data across different parallel computing nodes [HIL 86]. Often the same task is run on different data in parallel. Hybrid data/task parallelism is a parallel pipeline of tasks, each of which might be data parallel. Some of Big Data frameworks that utilize task parallelism are Apache Storm and Apache YARN (it supports more of hybrid parallelism, providing both task and data parallelism). Some of the Big Data frameworks that utilize data parallelism are Apache Spark, Apache MapReduce and Apache YARN.

3.2. Parallel metaheuristics

3.2.1. *General concepts*

Parallel metaheuristics can be used for the following reasons [TAL 09, TAL 15]:

– Speed up the search: one of the main goals of parallelizing a metaheuristic is to reduce the search time.

– Improve the quality of the solutions obtained.

– Improve the robustness: a parallel metaheuristic may be more robust than a non-parallel one in terms of solving in an effective manner different optimization problems and instances of a given problem.

– Solve large-scale problems: parallel metaheuristics allow us to solve large-scale instances of complex optimization problems by using task parallelism, for example. In Big Data, the challenge is often to solve very large instances that can be solved by a sequential machine.

There exists a large number of surveys on taxonomies of parallel metaheuristics. We can observe that there are two classical ways to present the concept of parallel metaheuristics: to view them in a metaheuristics point of view and divide the view in terms of single-based and population-based parallel metaheuristics [ALB 05, ALB 13, LUQ 11]. The other way is to have a more global taxonomy that takes into account both the algorithmic part and the parallel environment [TAL 09].

In the following section, the taxonomy of Alba *et al.* is used as it is the most illustrative one [ALB 05, ALB 13, LUQ 11].

3.2.2. *Parallel single solution-based metaheuristics*

Different parallel models have been proposed for single solution-based metaheuristics, and three of them are commonly used in the literature:

1) the parallel exploration and evaluation of the neighborhood (or parallel moves model);

2) the parallel multi-start model;

3) the parallel evaluation of a single solution (or move acceleration model).

3.2.2.1. *Parallel moves model*

This is a low-level master–slave model that does not alter the behavior of the technique. A sequential search would compute the same result but slowly. In the beginning of each iteration, the master duplicates the current solution between distributed nodes. Each one manages their candidate/solution and the application of the neighborhood operators separately. The results obtained are returned to the master.

3.2.2.2. *Parallel multi-start model*

This involves simultaneously launching several single solution-based metaheuristics for computing better and more robust solutions as several metaheuristics are used in the same time. The single solution-based metaheuristics may be heterogeneous or homogeneous, independent or cooperative, may start from the same or different solution(s) and may be configured with the same or different parameters.

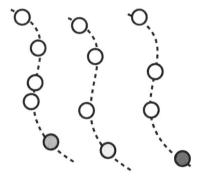

Figure 3.1. *Parallel multi-start model: several single solution-based metaheuristics are launched in parallel*

3.2.2.3. *Move acceleration model*

The quality of each move is evaluated in a parallel centralized way. This model is interesting to find whether the evaluation function can be parallelized as its CPU time-consuming and/or I/O intensive. In that case, the function can be viewed as an aggregation of a certain number of partial functions that can be run in parallel.

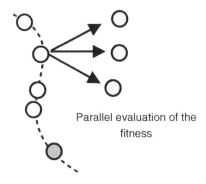

Figure 3.2. *Move acceleration model: the
solution is evaluated in parallel*

3.2.3. *Parallel population-based metaheuristics*

There are two ways of parallelism for population-based metaheuristics:

– Parallelization of computations: the operations applied commonly to each
of the individuals are performed in parallel.

– Parallelization of population: it this case, the population is split into
different parts that can be simply exchanged or evolved separately and then
joined later.

3.3. Infrastructure and technologies for parallel metaheuristics

3.3.1. *Distributed model*

3.3.1.1. *Parallel machine (cluster, network of workstation) computing*

In a network of workstations (NOW) or a cluster of workstations (COW),
workstations or PCs are interconnected using low-latency and high- bandwidth
interconnection networks.

3.3.1.2. *Grid computing*

Grid computers also tend to be more heterogeneous and geographically
dispersed (thus, not coupled physically) than cluster computers. One of the
main strategies of grid computing is to use middle-ware to divide and
apportion pieces of a program among several computers, sometimes up to
many thousands.

3.3.1.3. *Cloud computing*

Cloud computing is a model for enabling ubiquitous, convenient, on-demand access to a shared pool of configurable computing resources. It relies on sharing of resources to achieve coherence and economies of scale, similar to a utility (like the electricity grid) over a network.

Thanks to advanced software technologies allowing developers to build distributed processing more easily, metaheuristics are approaching Big Data. In particular, the use of one of the most popular distributed data processing technologies Apache Hadoop led metaheuristic to deal with real Big Data problems [FER 13, FER 15] in the case of feature selection. The Apache Hadoop software library http://hadoop.apache.org/ is a framework that allows for the distributed processing of large datasets across clusters of computers using simple programming models. It is designed to scale up from single servers to thousands of machines, each offering local computation and storage. Hadoop MapReduce is a software framework for easily writing applications that process vast amounts of data (multi-terabyte datasets) in parallel on large clusters (thousands of nodes) of commodity hardware in a reliable, fault-tolerant manner.

3.3.2. *Hardware model*

3.3.2.1. *GPU (graphics processing unit) computing*

GPU-accelerated computing is the use of a graphics processing unit (GPU) together with a CPU to accelerate scientific, analytics, engineering, consumer and enterprise applications. In GPGPU, the massive floating-point computational power of a GPU shader is turned into a very scalable computing resource for stream processing, capable of obtaining a significantly higher performance than the CPU. Actually, both modern supercomputers and desktop computers can take advantage of GPU acceleration, by using APIs (such as NVIDIA CUDA and GPL) to design parallel programs on GPU architectures.

More works focus on parallel metaheuristics on GPU: the first book on the subject [TSU 13] shows the increasing interest on the subject. In [KRÖ14], Kromer *et al.* provide an overview of some state-of-the-art research on the design, implementation and applications of parallel GA, DE, PSO and SA-based methods on the GPUs.

In [ROB 09], Robilliard *et al.* propose genetic programming (GP) on GPUs. In [LUO 13], authors introduce a new guideline for the design and implementation of effective local searches on GPU. Very efficient approaches are proposed for CPU-GPU data transfer optimization, thread control, mapping of neighboring solutions to GPU threads and memory management. [PED 13] propose a novel parallel optimization algorithm specially designed to run on GPUs. The underlying operation relates to systolic computing and is inspired by the systolic contraction of the heart that enables blood circulation. The algorithm, called systolic genetic search (SGS), is based on the synchronous circulation of solutions through a grid of processing units and tries to profit from the parallel architecture of GPUs to achieve high time performance. Frameworks like ParadisEO have been extended to work on GPU [MEL 13].

3.3.2.2. *APU (accelerated processing unit) computing*

An APU is a processor that includes both the CPU and GPU on a single chip. The name "APU" was coined by AMD, which released the first APU in January 2011. The APU takes parallel computing one step further by removing the bus between the CPU and GPU and integrating both units on the same chip. Since the bus is the main bottleneck in parallel processing, an APU is more efficient than a separate CPU and GPU.

Few works focus directly on metaheuristics on APU. In [MEN 13], Mentis *et al.* propose the design of a metaheuristic for achieving consensus among distributed autonomous agents based on the honeybee colony nest site selection process. Other authors design parallel MPSO variants with a genetic operator on APU [FRA 15].

3.3.2.3. *Multi-core computing*

Multi-core processor is a single computing component with two or more independent actual processing units (called "cores"), which are the units that read and execute program instructions. This hardware model is often used by researcher as it requires less effort than GPU or FPGA computing. In [RAG 11], three well-known metaheuristic algorithms with different ratios between independent calculations and shared memory usage are implemented and authors analyze the benefits of using multi-core CPUs compared with single-core CPUs. [NEB 10] propose a thread-based parallel version of MOEA/D designed to be executed on modern multi-core processors. An ant colony optimization metaheuristic on actual shared-memory parallel computers with the management of multiple colonies that use a global shared-memory to exchange information was also investigated in [DEL 09]. Recently, artificial bees have also been adapted to multi-core [SAN 12].

3.3.2.4. *FPGA (field programmable gate arrays) computing*

FPGA are programmable semiconductor devices (integrated circuit) that are based around a matrix of configurable logic blocks (CLBs) connected through programmable interconnects. FPGA can be configured by the user after manufacturing and hence they are field programmable. The FPGA configuration is generally specified using a hardware description language (HDL), similar to that used for an application-specific integrated circuit (ASIC).

Metaheuristics on FPGA are less recent than those on GPU and have appeared in the last two decades. In [SAL 05], three metaheuristic approaches are proposed for FPGA segmented channel routing problems (FSCRPs) with a new cost function, in which the cost of each assignment is not known in advance and the cost of a solution can only be obtained from entire feasible assignments. More recently, scatter search using Handel-C, a programming language for FPGA, is designed in [WAL 10] and (FPGA)-based parallel metaheuristic particle swarm optimization algorithm (PPSO) has been proposed in [HUA 13].

3.4. Quality measures

3.4.1. *Speedup*

Speedup is a metric for relative performance improvement when executing a task. Let S_p be the speedup for p processors, the speedup with p processors over a sequential system with a single processor can be defined as $S_p = \frac{T_1}{T_p}$, where T_1 is the time taken to run the program on a single processor system and T_p is the time taken to run the parallel program on p processors. Linear speedup or ideal speedup is obtained when $S_p = p$. When running an algorithm with linear speedup, doubling the number of processors doubles the speed. As this is ideal, it is considered very good scalability. Sometimes a speedup of more than p when using p processors is observed in parallel computing, which is called super-linear speedup.

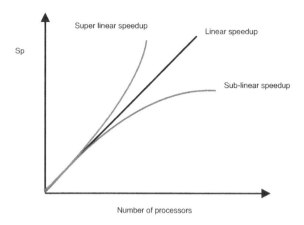

Figure 3.3. *Sub-linear, linear and super-linear speedup*

3.4.2. *Efficiency*

Efficiency is a performance metric defined as $E_p = \frac{S_p}{p} = \frac{T_1}{pT_p}$. It is a value, typically between zero and one, that estimates how well-utilized the processors are in solving the problem, compared with how much effort is wasted in communication and synchronization. Algorithms with linear speedup and algorithms running on a single processor have an efficiency of 1.

3.4.3. *Serial fraction*

The serial fraction of the algorithm measures the performance of any parallel algorithm that can help identify much more subtle effects than using speedup alone [KAR 90]. It is defined by $f_p = \frac{1/S_p - 1/p}{1 - 1/p}$.

3.5. Conclusion

As demonstrated in this chapter, parallelism and metaheuristics are interconnected. However, behind parallelism, several notions have to be defined: which parallelism, which infrastructure and what is the impact on the algorithmic part of the metaheuristic. Parallelism is a good solution to tackle Big Data, as it can offer calculation power quite easily but working directly on the algorithmic part of the problem could also help reduce the cost of computing.

4

Metaheuristics and Clustering

Clustering is one of the most commonly used descriptive tasks in data mining. It allows us to discover groups of similar objects in data where each group is called a cluster. Elements in one cluster are similar to one another and as different as possible from elements of other clusters. Several methods of clustering are effective at detecting different kinds of clusters.

In this chapter we first present the clustering task description. We then focus on how such a problem may be modeled as a combinatorial optimization problem is realized. As the search space is very large, many heuristics and, in particular, metaheuristics have been proposed to deal with this problem. A review of them is presented. Finally, a section is dedicated to the validation of the obtained clusters.

4.1. Task description

Clustering aims at grouping elements or objects into meaningful categories. Formally, given a set of n unlabeled examples $D = \{x(1), ..., x(n)\}$ in a d-dimensional feature space, D is partitioned into a number of disjoint subsets D_j, such that:

$$D = \cup_{j=1}^{k} D_j$$

where $D_i \cap D_j = \emptyset, i \neq j$ in which the points in each subset are similar to one another according to a given criterion ϕ. A partition is denoted by $\pi = (D_1, D_2, ..., D_k)$ and the problem of data clustering is thus formulated as:

$$\pi^* = argmin_\pi f(\pi)$$

where $f(.)$ is formulated according to ϕ.

A very good introduction to contemporary data mining clustering techniques can be found in the book of Han *et al.* [HAN 05a]. They divided clustering algorithms into different categories:

– partitioning methods (K-medoids Methods, K-means Methods, etc.);

– hierarchical methods (agglomerative algorithms, divisive algorithms, etc.);

– density-based algorithms (density-based connectivity clustering, density functions clustering);

– grid-based methods;

– methods based on co-occurrence of categorical data;

– constraint-based clustering;

– clustering algorithms used in machine learning and optimization;

– scalable clustering algorithms;

– algorithms for high dimensional data.

A lot of these methods are based on the notion of cluster dissimilarity that is obtained by an appropriate metric (often a distance measure between two elements). The choice of an appropriate metric will influence the shape of the clusters, as some elements can be closed with respect to a given measure, but distant relative to another one. Commonly used metrics are the Euclidian distance, the squared Euclidian distance, the Manhattan distance, Minkowski metric, the cosine, etc.

In the following, only standard algorithms are described.

4.1.1. *Partitioning methods*

In partition-based clustering, the objective is to partition a dataset into K disjoint sets of points, such that points of a set are as homogeneous as possible. Homogeneity is computed using a score function that is often based on a similarity notion or distance notion denoted by d. The objective is to minimize a function (average, sum, etc.) on the dissimilarity between each point and the centroid of the cluster it is assigned to. The centroid of a set could be an actual data point, or a "position" in the feature space. The most well-known algorithm of this category is K-means [MAC 67] presented in Algorithm 4.1. In its most basic version, this algorithm begins by randomly picking K cluster centers and then labeling each point according to its nearest cluster center. Once each point is labeled, a new cluster center can be calculated according to the centroid of each labeled cluster. The algorithm then iterates until there is no longer change of the cluster centers.

Algorithm 4.1. Classical K-means algorithm

> **for** k=1 to K
> let $r(k)$ be a randomly chosen point from D **do**
> **end for**
> **while** changes in clusters C_k happen **do**
>   **for** k=1, ..., K **do**
> $C_k = \{x \in D \, d(r(k), x) \leq d(r(j), x) \text{ for all } j = 1...K, j \neq k\}$
>   **end for**
>   **for** k=1,...,K **do**
>   compute new center r_k vector mean of the points in C_k
>   **end for**
> **end while**

There are several variants of the K-means algorithm, for example:

– k-medians clustering [JAI 88] uses the median in each dimension instead of the mean;

– k-medoids [KAU 87] and partitioning around medoids (PAM) use the medoid instead of the mean;

– fuzzy C-means clustering [NOC 06] is a soft version of K-means, where each data point has a fuzzy degree of belonging to each cluster.

4.1.2. *Hierarchical methods*

There exist two distinct types of hierarchical methods: the agglomerative ones, which start with singleton clusters and gradually merge them, and the divisive ones, which begin with all the data in a single cluster and gradually divide it into smaller clusters. The agglomerative methods are the most widely used methods. Hierarchical methods of cluster analysis allow a convenient graphical display in which the entire sequence of merging (or splitting) of clusters is shown. Because of its tree-like structure, the resulting display is called a dendrogram (see Figure 4.1).

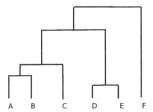

Figure 4.1. *An example of dendrogram*

Agglomerative methods are based on measures of distance between clusters and are described in Algorithm 4.2. They iteratively merge the two closest clusters to reduce the number of clusters. Usually, the starting configuration of the process consists of each point in its own cluster. Then, the merging is realized until a single cluster containing all the data points is obtained. Different distance measures between clusters have been proposed and lead to different algorithms: for example, the single-link hierarchical clustering algorithm merges the two clusters with the smallest minimum pairwise distance. Another variant is the complete-link hierarchical clustering algorithm, where the two clusters with the smallest maximum pairwise distance are merged.

Divisive methods begin with a single cluster that contains all the data points and split it into subsets. The process of splitting is iterated as far as necessary and ends with singleton clusters.

Algorithm 4.2. Agglomerative methods

---

for i=1, ..., n **do**
   while There is more than one cluster left **do**
      for k=1, ..., K **do**
         Let C_i and C_j be the clusters minimizing the distance $D(C_K, C_h)$
         between any two clusters
         $C_i = C_i \cup C_j$
         Remove cluster C_j
      end for
   end while
end for

4.1.3. *Grid-based methods*

Density-based and/or grid-based approaches are popular for mining clusters in a large multidimensional space wherein clusters are regarded as denser regions than their surroundings. The grid-based clustering approach differs from the conventional clustering algorithms, in that it is concerned not with the data points but with the value space that surrounds the data points. The grid-based clustering algorithm consists of five basic steps [GRA 02]:

1) creating the grid structure, i.e. partitioning the data space into a finite number of cells;

2) calculating the cell density for each cell;

3) ranking of the cells according to their densities;

4) identifying cluster centers;

5) traversal of neighbor cells.

The main advantage of this approach is its fast processing time because it goes through the dataset once to compute the statistical values for the grids.

4.1.4. *Density-based methods*

Density-based methods assume that the points that belong to each cluster are drawn from a specific probability distribution. The overall distribution of the data is assumed to be a mixture of several distributions. The aim of these methods is to identify the clusters and their distribution parameters. These methods are designed for discovering clusters of arbitrary shapes that are not necessarily convex. DBSCAN (density-based spatial clustering of applications with noise), which uses the concept of density reachability and density connectivity, is the most well-known density-based clustering algorithm [EST 96]. A point, p, is said to be density reachable from a point, q, if p is within ϵ distance from point q and q has a sufficient number of points in its neighbors that are within distance ϵ. A point p and q are said to be density connected if there exists a point r that has a sufficient number of points in its neighbors and both the p and q are within the ϵ distance. This is a chain process from r. So, if q is neighbor of r, r is neighbor of s, s is neighbor of t which, in turn, is neighbor of p, then it implies that q is neighbor of p.

4.2. Big Data and clustering

In their review, dedicated to clustering in a context of Big Data, Fahad *et al.* proposed a categorizing taxonomy to classify a number of clustering algorithms [FAH 14]. They performed an empirical study that allowed them to draw some conclusions in the context of Big Data:

– Some clustering algorithms show excellent performance with respect to the quality of the clustering outputs, except for high-dimensional data. However, these algorithms suffer from high computational time requirements.

– All clustering algorithms suffer from a stability problem. To mitigate such an issue, ensemble clustering should be considered.

– No clustering algorithm performs well for all the evaluation criteria, and future work should be dedicated to address the drawbacks of each clustering algorithm accordingly.

4.3. Optimization model

In parallel to the standard methods presented above, some contributions to clustering deal with combinatorial optimization approaches. Hence this section presents how a clustering problem may be modeled as a combinatorial optimization problem. Particular attention is given to the quality measures that may represent the optimization criterion.

4.3.1. *A combinatorial problem*

In the following definition, we only consider non-fuzzy clustering, i.e. each data point belongs to one and only one cluster, which is also called hard clustering. The clustering problem can be expressed as follows.

Given a set of n data points $D = \{x(1), ..., x(n)\}$ described by n features, the objective is to affect each data point $x(i)$ to a unique cluster C_i, such that $D = \cup_{i=1}^{k} C_i$, $C_i \neq \emptyset$ (non-null cluster), $C_i \cap C_j = \emptyset$ for $i \neq j$ and such that a quality function f is optimized. Depending on the problem, the number k can be set or should be found by the optimization method.

Clustering is then a combinatorial problem as the data points or objects have to be affected to fix or not number of clusters. The number of combinations can be very large. When the number of clusters k is fixed, the number of combinations to assign the n data points is $S(n, k) = \frac{1}{k!} \sum_{i=0}^{k} (-1)^{k-1} \binom{k}{i} i^n$ and the search space size in finding the optimal number of clusters is $B(n) = \sum_{k=1}^{n} S(n, k)$. S is known as the Stirling number and B the Bell numbers.

There also exists *soft clustering* where each object fully belongs to one or several clusters or *fuzzy clustering* where each object belongs to one or more clusters with different degrees.

There exist several quality functions that can be optimized and they have often the objective to construct well-separated and compact clusters. Some objective functions are detailed in the following section.

4.3.2. *Quality measures*

Quality measures for clustering are often statistical-mathematical functions based on the notion of similarity or distance/dissimilarity between the data points. They include the internal cluster validity index. These functions often have the objective of:

– *Compactness:* data points in one cluster should be as similar as possible to the each other.

– *Separation:* clusters should be well separated and can be measured, for example, by inter-cluster measures.

Table 4.1 presents an overview of the most widely used objective functions and their category of objective.

Objective functions	Class
Variance	Compactness
Deviation	Compactness
Total symmetrical compactness	Compactness
Global compactness	Compactness
Global cluster variance	Compactness
Connectivity	Separation
Separation-based centroid clusters	Separation
Min dist(2 centroid)	Separation
Complete link	Separation
Single link	Separation
Negative Ratio Association	Compactness
J'_{FWSC}	Compactness
Ratio Cut	Separation
XB	Separation
SSXB	Ratio (compactness/separation)
DB	Compactness + separation
Si	Compactness + separation

Table 4.1. *Most widely used objective functions and their category*

4.3.2.1. *Compactness*

The first category of quality measures belongs to compactness measure. The most widely used in the literature of this category are variance and deviation.

4.3.2.1.1. Variance

The variance objective function is a compactness objective function. The variance is a measure of how far a set of data points is spread out [BAN 07, HAN 04, HAN 12]. It is computed as:

$$Var(C) = \sum_{C_k \in C} \sum_{i \in C_k} d(i, c_k)^2$$

where C is a set of clusters, c_k is a cluster center of C_k and $d(...)$ is a distance function to be defined. The variance is an objective function to minimize.

4.3.2.1.2. Deviation

The deviation objective function [HAN 07a, HAN 12] is mostly the same as the variance, which expresses the cluster compactness. To compute the deviation, the distance between data and their cluster center are summed.

$$Dev(C) = \sum_{C_k \in C} \sum_{i \in C_k} d(i, c_k)$$

Let us note that the difference between deviation and variance is that, in variance, the distance is a square distance.

4.3.2.1.3. Total symmetrical compactness

The total symmetrical compactness objective function measures the total symmetrical distance [YIF 12] within a cluster. It is computed as the overall summed point symmetry (PS) distance between data points and their corresponding cluster center. It is defined as:

$$TSC(C) = \sum_{C_k \in C} \sum_{i \in C_k} d_{ps}(i, c_k)$$

where $d_{ps}(i, c_k)$ is the distance PS between i and the centroid c_k computed as follows:

$$d_{ps}(i, c_k) = (nn_{i'(1)} + nn_{i'(2)})/2 \times d_e(i, c_k)$$

where $d_e(i, c_k)$ is the Euclidean distance between data i and the centroid c_k, i' is the symmetric point of i relatively to the center c_k and $nn_{i'(1)}$ and $nn_{i'(2)}$ are, respectively, the first and second nearest neighbors of i'. i' can, for example, be computed by $2 \times c_k - i$.

4.3.2.1.4. Global compactness

The global compactness objective function has been presented in [MUK 11]. The global compactness is a ratio variation on fuzzy cardinality. It is defined as variation:

$$\sigma_k = \sum_{i=1}^{N} u_{ik} d_e(c_k, x_i), \qquad 1 \le k \le K$$

Fuzzy cardinality:

$$n_k = \sum_{i=1}^{N} u_{ik}, \qquad 1 \le k \le K$$

Global compactness :

$$GC(C) = \sum_{k=1}^{K} \frac{\sigma_k}{n_k} = \sum_{k=1}^{K} \frac{\sum_{i=1}^{N} u_{ik} d_e(c_k, x_i)}{\sum_{i=1}^{N} u_{ik}}$$

where N is the number of data points, x_i is the ith data of the datasets and u_{ik} denotes the membership degree of the ith categorical object to the kth cluster, and the size of this matrix is $N \times K$. This matrix contains values in the interval [0;1] and is computed as:

$$u_{ik} = \frac{1}{\sum_{l=1}^{K} \left(\frac{d_e(c_k, x_i)}{d_e(c_l, x_i)} \right)^{\frac{1}{m-1}}}$$

where m is the fuzzy exponent, $m \in]1; +\infty]$.

4.3.2.1.5. Connectivity

The connectivity compactness objective function evaluates the degree to which neighboring data points have been placed in the same cluster [HAN 07a, HAN 12, YIF 12] and is the most widely used in the literature. It is computed as:

$$Conn(C) = \frac{1}{N} \sum_{i=1}^{N} \left(\frac{\sum_{j=1}^{h} \omega_{i,nn_i(j)}}{h} \right)$$

where

$$\omega_{a,b} = \begin{cases} 1 \text{ if } \exists C_k | a, b \in C_k \\ 0 \text{ otherwise.} \end{cases}$$

with $nn_{i(j)}$ being the jth nearest neighbor of the data i, h being the number of neighbors used to compute the connectivity and N being the number of data points. The value of connectivity lies in the interval $[0, 1]$. This objective should be maximized.

4.3.2.1.6. Global cluster variance

The global cluster variance objective function is computed with the fuzzy C-means (FCM) algorithm, which a widely used technique that uses the principles of fuzzy sets to evolve a partition matrix $U(X)$ while minimizing the measure [SAH 11]:

$$GCV(C) = \sum_{j=1}^{N} \sum_{k=1}^{K} u_{kj}^m d_e(c_k, x_j)^2$$

FCM algorithm starts with random initial K cluster centers, and then at every iteration it finds the fuzzy membership of each data point to every cluster using the following equation:

$$u_{ik} = \frac{(1/d_e(c_k, x_i))^{\frac{1}{(m-1)}}}{\sum_{j=1}^{k}(1/d_e(c_j, x_i))^{\frac{1}{(m-1)}}}$$

4.3.2.2. *Separation*

After the presentation of the compactness objective functions, the most widely used separation objective functions of the literature are presented. The aim of these measures is to evaluate whether distant elements are in different clusters.

4.3.2.2.1. Separation-based centroid clusters

The separation-based centroid clusters objective function allows us to compute the global sum between clusters centroids [HAN 12, MUK 09]. It is computed as:

$$SumD(C) = \sum_{C_k \in C, C_l \in C, l \neq k} d(c_k, c_l)$$

where c_k and c_l are the cluster centroids of clusters C_k and C_l, respectively.

4.3.2.2.2. Minimum distance between cluster centroids

Another separation objective function is proposed in [BAN 07, HAN 12]. This objective function is used to maximize the minimum distance between two cluster centroids. It is computed as:

$$Dmin(C) = \min_{C_k \in C, \, C_l \in C, l \neq k} d(c_k, c_l)$$

where c_k and c_l are the cluster centroids of clusters C_k and C_l, respectively.

4.3.2.2.3. Complete link

The complete link objective function is described in [HAN 78]. Complete link computes the distance between two clusters. It is defined by the maximum distance between two data points that are not in the same cluster:

$$CL(C_i, C_j) = \max_{C_i \in C, C_j \in C} d(i, j)$$

where i and j are data belonging to the clusters C_i and C_j, respectively.

4.3.2.2.4. Single link

The single link objective function is described in [HAN 78]. Single link is similar to complete link. It defines the distance between two clusters by the minimum distance between two data points that are not in the same cluster:

$$SL(C_i, C_j) = \min_{C_i \in C, C_j \in C} d(i, j)$$

where i and j are data belonging to the clusters C_i and C_j, respectively.

4.3.2.3. *Compactness and separation measure*

Some measures attempt to combine the two important properties for clustering, they are as follows.

4.3.2.3.1. Davies-Bouldin (DB) index

In the Davies–Bouldin index [DAV 79], the cohesion is estimated by the mean distance of the objects to their respective centroid and the separation quantifies the distance between centroids.

4.3.2.3.2. Calinski–Harabasz index (CH)

The Calinski–Harabasz index is a ratio-type index in which the cohesion is estimated by the sum of the distances of the patterns to their respective centroid and the separation is measured by the sum of the distances from each centroid to the global prototype [GAR 12].

4.3.2.3.3. Silhouette index (Si)

The Silhouette index is a normalized summation-type index in which the cohesion is measured by the sum of the distances between all the points in the same cluster and the separation is based on the nearest-neighbor distance between points in different groups [ROU 87].

4.3.2.3.4. Turi index (TI)

The Turi index is a ratio-type index where the inter-cluster separation is estimated by the minimum distance between centroids and the intra-cluster dispersion is computed by the average distance between each object and its respective centroid [GAR 12].

4.3.2.3.5. Weight of evidence information

The weight of evidence information is an uncertainty measure based on mutual information, which estimates the amount of evidence information between an object and a cluster at a given confidence level [GIL 90].

4.3.2.4. *Multi-objective models*

The clustering problem is natively bi-objective and can even be multi-objective. In multi-objective clustering, the aim is to decompose a dataset into similar groups maximizing multiple objectives in parallel. Often the authors take a combination of two quality measures: one to optimize separation and another to optimize compactness. Figure 4.2 illustrates an example where both objectives are optimized either independently or simultaneously [GAR 12].

The multi-objective clustering allows us to find a solution by using multi-objective approaches. It evaluates each objective simultaneously for each clustering solution. As a result, the clustering solutions are stored in a collection of solutions where each one represents a different trade-off among objectives (see Figure 4.3).

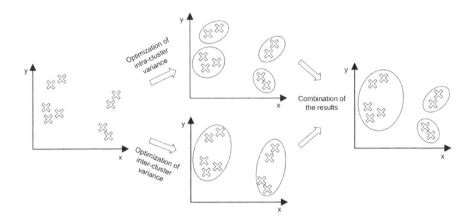

Figure 4.2. *Optimizing both objectives simultaneously [GAR 12]*

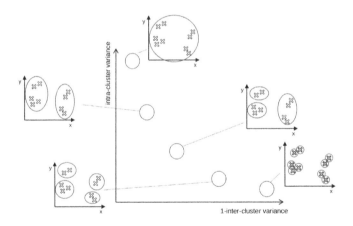

Figure 4.3. *Multi-objective clustering a Pareto set*
of solutions [GAR 12]

4.3.3. *Representation*

In metaheuristics, several representations are used for clustering. They depend on the nature of the clustering problem: is its number of clusters fixed or not?

4.3.3.1. *Fixed number of clusters*

4.3.3.1.1. Binary encoding

In a binary encoding, a clustering solution (partition) is usually represented as k binary strings of length N, where N is the number of data points. In this $k \times N$ matrix, the rows represent clusters and the columns represent objects. In this case, if the object j belongs to the cluster i, then 1 is assigned to the ith element of the jth column of the solution, whereas the other elements of the same column receive 0 (see Figure 4.4).

In cluster prototype binary encoding, each clustering solution is represented as a binary string of length n and the value of the ith position is "1" if the ith object is considered as a cluster prototype and "0" otherwise (see Figure 4.5).

Object

1	2	3	4	5	6	7	8	9	10

Encoding

1	1	1	1	0	0	0	0	0	0
0	0	1	0	1	1	1	1	0	0
0	0	0	0	0	0	0	0	1	1

Clustering

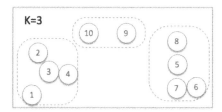

Figure 4.4. *Binary encoding with a fixed number of clusters from [JOS 16]*

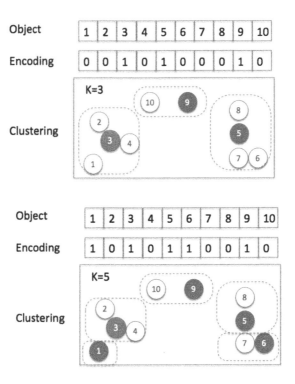

Figure 4.5. *Binary encoding for representative from [JOS 16]*

4.3.3.1.2. Integer encoding

There are two ways of representing clustering solutions by means of integer encoding. In the first one, an element (position) of the solution is an integer vector of N elements. Each position corresponds to a particular object, i.e. the ith position represents the ith dataset object. Given that a solution represents a partition formed by k clusters, each gene has a value over the alphabet $\{1, 2, 3,..., k\}$. These values define the cluster labels, thus leading to a *label-based representation*. Figure 4.6 shows the examples of this representation.

The second possibility uses an array of k elements to provide a *medoid-based representation* of the dataset. In this case, each array element represents the index of the object x_i, $i = 1, 2, ..., N$ (with respect to the order the objects appear in the dataset) corresponding to the prototype of a given cluster.

4.3.3.1.3. Real encoding

In real encoding, a solution is a vector of real numbers that represent the coordinates of the cluster prototypes. The population-based metaheuristics used in automatic clustering commonly uses fixed- or variable-length real encoding. In fixed-length encoding, all clustering solutions encode a predefined maximum number of prototypes, K_{max}. Hence all members of the population maintain the same length throughout the optimization process. However, in variable-length encoding, the population-based metaheuristics should adjust the search operators to cope with members of different sizes [JOS 16].

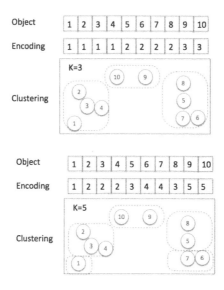

Figure 4.6. *Integer encoding: label-based representation from [JOS 16]*

4.3.3.2. *With variable numbers of clusters*

Most of the encodings used in the previous section can also be used when the number of clusters is unknown but some are specific:

– locus-based adjacency representation [HAN 05b];

– prototype-based representation (represents the centroid or the medoid or the mode of the clusters);

– label-based representation (represents the number of the clusters).

4.3.3.2.1. Locus-based adjacency representation

In the locus-based adjacency graph representation, each solution consists of n elements (genes for a GA), where n is the number of data points. Each element can have integer values in $\{1, ..., n\}$. If element i is assigned a value j that represents a link between the data points i and j and in the resulting clustering solution, these two points will belong to the same cluster (see Figure 4.7). Therefore, for decoding the solution, it is required to identify all the connected components of the graph. This representation is suitable to find both the number of clusters and the affectation of the points to the clusters.

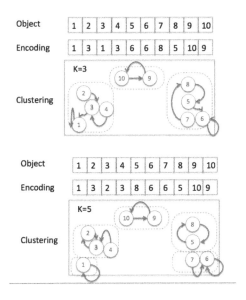

Figure 4.7. *Integer encoding: graph-based representation from [JOS 16]*

4.3.3.3. *Operators*

Operators are very classical for all the representations. For prototype-based encoding, the crossovers used are single-point, two-point, centroid-pool and exchanging prototype. For label-based encoding, the authors use single point and uniform crossover. For mutation or neighborhood in local searches, they are more dependent on the representation. Mutation for prototype-based encoding can be the following: a cluster centroid perturbation with either use of uniform distribution, Gaussian distribution, polynomial distribution, log-normal distribution; a cluster medoid replacement; a categorical value replacement. For label-based encoding, the mutation can be directed neighborhood, probability-based replacement and random replacement. For the adjacency graph encoding, the directed neighborhood is used.

4.4. Overview of methods

There are many surveys on metaheuristics for clustering [NAN 14, HRU 09, JOS 16] and some of them focus, in particular, on multi-objective clustering [KUR 13, MUK 15, BON 11]. Some surveys focus only on genetic algorithms or evolutionary algorithms [SHE 08], whereas others propose a specific survey on swarm intelligence for clustering [HAN 07b, RAN 10, ALA 14].

Metaheuristic	Algo.	Reference	Encoding	Objective function
GA	HEA	[LAI 09]	B	Var
GA	KMQGA	[XIA 10]	C-VL	DB
GA	CGA	[HRU 04]	L	SI
PSO	DCPSO	[OMR 06]	C-FL	TI
ACO	ATTA-C	[HAN 06]	C-FL	NF

Table 4.2. *Summary table of the some single objective algorithms for hard clustering. C = centroid-based encoding, VL = variable length, FL = fixed length, B = binary encoding*

In [NAN 14], authors focus particularly on partitioning methods with single objective-based metaheuristics. We can note the large number of genetic algorithms based on clustering algorithms with a fixed number of clusters [BEZ 94, SAR 97, MUR 96, MAU 00, KRI 99] or not [COW 99, TSE 01, BAN 01]. ACO are also used as in [SHE 04, XU 04, GHO 08, GAO 16]. Other paradigms of metaheuristics are also used and more and more interest is shown to differential evolution (DE).

Table 4.2 gives a short overview of single objective algorithms.

Bong and Rajeswari [BON 11] reported that the algorithm design, development and applications of multi-objective nature-inspired metaheuristics for clustering and classification increased notably during the years 2006–2010. In the literature, there are many works on multi-objective clustering. One of the first multi-objective clustering (MOC) approaches was

VIENNA, introduced by Handl and Knowles based on PESA-II, incorporating specialized mutation and initialization procedure [HAN 04]. This algorithm requires us to know *a priori* the number of clusters.

Table 4.3 presents the most famous multi-objective clustering methods observed in the literature. More examples can be found in [MUK 15]. Table 4.3 indicates for each of them:

– the name and references of the multi-objective algorithm;

– whether the number of clusters k is fixed;

– the type of representation used;

– the pair of objective functions proposed;

– crossover and mutation operators defined;

– datasets used to validate the approach.

By analyzing this table, we can see that some components are mentioned several times, this is the case of locus-based adjacency representation, of objective functions like variance and connectivity or mutation based on nearest neighbors.

4.5. Validation

In supervised classification, the evaluation of the classification model obtained is a part of the process of developing a classification model and there are some well-accepted evaluation measures and methodology but, in clustering, it is not the case. Tan and Kumar proposed a list of issues that are important for cluster validation [TAN 05]:

1) determining the clustering tendency of a set of data, i.e. distinguishing whether non-random structure exists in the data;

2) determining the correct number of clusters;

3) evaluating how well the results fit the data without reference to external information;

4) comparing the results of a cluster analysis to externally known results, such as externally provided class labels;

5) comparing two sets of clusters to determine which is better.

Algorithms/References	k fixed ?	Representation	Objective functions	Operators	MO-Algo
VIENNA [HAN 04]	Yes	Label-based Voronoi Cells	– Variance – Connectivity	– No crossover – Directed mutation-based NN	PESA-II
MOCK [HAN 07a, HAN 12]	No	Locus-based adjacency	– Deviation – Connectivity	– Uniform crossover – Nearest-neighbors mutation	PESA-II
SiMM-TS [BAN 07]	No	– Eisen plot – Cluster profile plot	– Variance – min dist(2 centroids)	crossover and mutation (unknown)	MOGA (NSGA II)
MOGA [MUK 07]	No	Centroid-based	– Silhouette Index – Variance	Single point Xover Centroid perturbation mutation	NSGA II
MOGA-Based Fuzzy Clustering of Categorical Attributes [MUK 09]	No	Chromosome representation	– Global compactness – Separation	selection – Single point crossover – Random mutation	NSGA II
MOSSC [ZHU 12]	No	Chromosome representation	– SSXB – J_{fwsc}	– Binary tournament - crowded comparison operator based – Simulated binary crossover – Polynomial mutation	
MOEA/D-Net [GON 12]	No	Locus-based adjacency	– Negative Ratio Association – Ratio Cut	– 2-points crossover – Neighbor-based mutation	
MOMoDEFC [SAH 11]	No	Vector	– XB – Global cluster variance	– MoDE crossover – modiMutation	
MOVGA [MUK 11]	No	Centroid-based	– Global compactness – Separation based centroid clusters	– Crowded binary tournament selection – crossover point – random mutation	NSGA II
MGEPC [YIF 12]	No	?	– Total symmetrical compactness – Connectivity	– Binary tournament selection – mutation randomly	

Table 4.3. Summary table of the most famous multi-objective clustering methods

Items 1, 2 and 3 will use internal information only to provide quality information on the clusters provided, whereas item 4 will use external information.

4.5.1. *Internal validation*

Many internal measures of cluster validity for partitional clustering are based on compactness/cohesion or separation. These measures are often used as objective functions in the clustering algorithms and summed up in section 4.3.2. In general, the validity of a clustering is a weighted sum of the validity of individual clusters.

4.5.2. *External validation*

External validation is often based on class labels of the data objects. The usual methodology is then to measure the degree of correspondence between the cluster labels and the class labels. More formally, external validation techniques allow us to compare two given partitions G and H. G corresponds to a clustering solution obtained and H corresponds to a theoretical solution or the real solution, if possible. Using these two partitions, it is possible to obtain a contingency table. The contingency table is a type of table in a matrix format that displays the frequency distribution of the variables. This table is computed as:

$$a = |\{i, j | C_{G(i)} = C_{G(j)} \wedge C_{H(i)} = C_{H(j)}\}|$$

$$b = |\{i, j | C_{G(i)} = C_{G(j)} \wedge C_{H(i)} \neq C_{H(j)}\}|$$

$$c = |\{i, j | C_{G(i)} \neq C_{G(j)} \wedge C_{H(i)} = C_{H(j)}\}|$$

$$d = |\{i, j | C_{G(i)} \neq C_{G(j)} \wedge C_{H(i)} \neq C_{H(j)}\}|$$

The values a, b, c and d are computed for each possible pair of data elements i and j and their respective cluster assignments $C_{G(i)}$, $C_{G(j)}$, $C_{H(i)}$ and $C_{H(j)}$.

4.5.2.1. *Classification measures*

There are a large number of measures that are used to evaluate a classification model. Some of them include entropy, purity, precision, recall and F-measure. These measures are presented in Chapter 7.

In the following, we detail measures that are based on the premise that any two objects that are in the same cluster should be in the same class and vice versa.

4.5.2.2. Rand index

The Rand index validation technique [HAN 05b] is based on counting the number of pairwise co-assignments of data elements. The Rand index is defined as:

$$RI(G, H) = \frac{a + d}{M}$$

where M is the number of possible pairs $(a + b + c + d)$. The Rand index is between 0 and 1 and should be maximized, when the two partitions agree perfectly, the Rand index is 1.

4.5.2.3. Adjusted Rand index

A problem with the Rand index is that the expected value of the Rand index of two random partitions does not take a constant value (say zero). The adjusted Rand index assumes the generalized hyper-geometric distribution as the model of randomness, i.e. the G and H partitions are picked at random, such that the number of objects in the classes and clusters are fixed. The adjusted Rand index is computed as [GAR 12]:

$$ARI(G, H) = \frac{a - [(a + b)(a + c)]/2}{[(a + b) + (a + c)]/2 - [(a + b)(a + c)]/d}$$

The adjusted Rand index is between 0 and 1 which should be maximized.

4.5.2.4. Jaccard coefficient

The Jaccard coefficient [GAR 12] is a statistical measure used for comparing the similarity and diversity of sample sets. This coefficient is computed as:

$$J(G, H) = \frac{a}{a + b + c}$$

4.5.2.5. *Fowlkes and Mallows index*

The Fowlkes–Mallows index [GAR 12] is an external evaluation method that is used to determine the similarity between two clusterings (clusters obtained after a clustering algorithm). This measure of similarity could be either between two hierarchical clustering or a clustering and a benchmark classification. A higher value for the Fowlkes–Mallows index indicates a greater similarity between the clusters and the benchmark classifications. This index is computed as:

$$FM(G, H) = \sqrt{\frac{a}{a+b} \times \frac{a}{a+c}}$$

4.6. Conclusion

In this chapter, we have presented an overview of clustering algorithms. Several methods exist to deal with clustering and metaheuristics, particularly multi-objective metaheuristics are more widely used. Big Data is still challenging for clustering as many classical approaches are based on an exhaustive computation of distance between data points or representatives, the conventional approaches cannot be applied. Therefore, metaheuristics and, in particular, parallel metaheuristics could be a very interesting solution to the faced explosion of data.

5

Metaheuristics and Association Rules

Association rules mining is a widely used approach for discovering interesting relationships between columns (variables/attributes) of large databases. The first applications for such an approach dealt with the *market-basket analysis* problem, where the aim is to identify a set of items (columns of the database) frequently purchased simultaneously in the same transaction (rows of the database). Since this first application, many other problems have been studied including web usage mining, intrusion detection, continuous production and bioinformatics. Indeed, association rules are a very general model and may overcome some drawbacks of other classical knowledge discovery tasks such as classification. For example, an association rule can be considered as a general case of a classification rule as in association rules, the consequent may consist of a set of attributes, and is not limited to a single one. Let us note that in contrast to sequence mining, association rules learning does not consider the order of items.

In this chapter we first present the task description. Then, we show how such a problem may be modeled as a combinatorial optimization problem. As the search space is very large, many heuristics and particularly metaheuristics have been proposed to deal with this problem. A review of these metaheuristics is presented. This review first provides some generalities and then considers each type of association rules (qualitative, quantitative and fuzzy) separately.

5.1. Task description and classical approaches

5.1.1. *Initial problem*

Historically, the problem of discovering association rules was first formulated in [AGR 93] and called the market-basket problem. The initial problem was as follows: given a set of items and a large collection of sales records, which consist of a transaction date and the items purchased in that transaction, the task is to find significant relationships between the items contained in different transactions. Following this first application, association rules may now be defined in a more general way. Let us consider a database composed of transactions (records or objects) described according to several – maybe many – attributes (features or columns). Association rules provide a very simple, but useful, way to present correlations or other relationships among attributes (features) expressed in the form $C \Rightarrow P$ (or *IF C THEN P*), where C is the condition part (antecedent) and P is the prediction part (consequent). C and P are disjoint sets of attributes. Both the C and P parts contain a conjunction of different terms indicating specific values for specific attributes. Hence the general form of an association rule is:

$$IF \ < term_1 > \ and \ ... \ < term_p > \ THEN$$

$$< term_{p+1} > \ and \ ... \ < term_n >$$

where $< term_i >$ is of the form $< attribute_i = value_{i_j} >$.

Let us note that most of the time, the prediction part is composed of a single term only. Hence the rule has the following form:

$$IF \ < term_1 > \ and \ < term_2 > \ and \ ... \ < term_p > \ THEN \ < term_n >$$

Moreover, when the prediction part is composed of a specific term to predict (the same for all the rules), the association rule becomes a classification rule of the form:

$$IF \ < term_1 > \ and \ < term_2 > \ and \ ... \ < term_p > \ THEN \ Class,$$

Classification rules can be seen as a straightforward classification task and will be presented in the chapter dealing with classification, although models and methods used for this task are for some points very close to those used more generally in rule mining.

5.1.2. *A priori algorithm*

The best-known algorithm to mine association rules is *a priori*, proposed by Agrawal and Srikant [AGR 94]. It is based on the notion of *frequent item sets* that are sets of items – or attributes – that often occur together within transactions and respect a minimum level of *support*. Hence the *a priori* algorithm finds in a two-phase approach all frequent item sets that have at least a given minimum level of *confidence*. *Support* and *confidence* are widely used metrics. They are defined later in this chapter.

While the second phase (looking for rules with high level of *confidence*) is straightforward, the first phase needs to be considered carefully. Finding all frequent item sets may be difficult as it involves searching all possible item sets (combination of items). The number of possible item sets, when n items are available, is in the order of 2^{n-1}. Although the number of possible item sets increases exponentially with n, an efficient search exploiting the downward closure property of *support* may be used. This property guarantees that given a frequent item set, all its subsets are also frequent and thus for an infrequent item set, all its supersets must also be infrequent. Exploiting this property, *a priori* efficiently uses a breadth-first search to enumerate frequent item sets. It constructs frequent item sets of size k, combining those of size $k - 1$.

Such an algorithm suffers of several drawbacks. Perhaps the most important one is that the whole database has to be scanned several times to construct the item sets. Hence many improvements on the initial method, as well as efficient implementations (including parallel implementations), have been proposed to deal with very large databases [ZAK 01, BOR 03, YE 06].

Another drawback of this approach is the role played by the *support* measure. Allowing us to identify low support rules generates a huge number of rules that are difficult to interpret. However, low support rules may still be an interesting information as rare rules may be very important in some application contexts (for example, medical applications). In this sense, other types of approaches, using different quality measures, have to be proposed. Optimization approaches and particularly the multi-objective optimization approaches are very suitable to deal with several kinds of measures and can overcome this drawback. As the search space that is composed of all the combinations of attributes is huge, metaheuristics have been widely used to deal with this problem.

5.2. Optimization model

Before considering alternative methods proposed to deal with the association rules problem, this section first shows how this problem can be modeled as a combinatorial optimization problem.

5.2.1. *A combinatorial problem*

The task of discovering effective association rules may be seen as a combinatorial optimization problem, since rules are combinations of terms, where each term involves a different attribute. Hence each attribute can belong to the rule in the antecedent or the consequent part. Each attribute has several possible values forming as many possible terms. When the number of attributes is very large (up to several thousands), the number of possible rules (choice of the attributes that belong to the rule and their values) is exponentially large. Therefore, efficient methods capable of dealing with such large size problems (heuristic approaches and particularly metaheuristic approaches) are needed.

5.2.2. *Quality measures*

Association rules mining has been widely studied in the literature, but usually only frequent patterns are sought (as in the *a priori* approach). However, depending on the application context, *interesting* associations are not only the frequent ones. A lot of measures exist for estimating the quality of association rules. For an overview, readers can refer to Freitas [FRE 99], Tan *et al.* [TAN 02], Geng and Hamilton [GEN 06] and Hilderman *et al.* [HIL 13], among others. In the context of knowledge discovery in medical data, for example, Ohsaki *et al.* proposed some measures [OHS 07]. Some of these quality measures are presented in Table 5.1.

Formulas are given for a set of N instances, where $|C|$ represents the number of instances satisfying the C part of the rule, $|P|$ the number of instances satisfying the P part of the rule and $|C \ and \ P|$ is the number of instances satisfying simultaneously the C and P parts of the rule. $Pr(C)$ is the probability of occurences of C. In the JFmeasure, N_{pu} is the number of potentially useful attributes of the C part of the rule and NT the total number of attributes of the C part. and $w2$ are two user-specified parameters chosen between 0 and 1.

Measure	Formula
Support (S)	$S = \frac{|C\ and\ P|}{N}$
Confidence ($Conf$)	$Conf = \frac{|Cf\ and\ P|}{|C|}$
Laplace (L)	$L = \frac{|C\ and\ P|+1}{|C|+2}$
Interest (I)	$I = \frac{N*|C\ and\ P|}{|C|*|P|}$
Conviction (V)	$V = \frac{|C|*|\overline{P}|}{N*|C\ and\ \overline{P}|}$
Surprise (R)	$R = \frac{|C\ and\ P|-|Cand\overline{P}|}{|\overline{P}|}$
Jaccard (ζ)	$\zeta = \frac{|C\ and\ P|}{|C|+|P|-|C\ and\ P|}$
Phi-coefficient (ϕ)	$\phi^2 = \frac{(|C\ and\ P|*|\overline{C}\ and\ \overline{P}|-|C\ and\ P|*|\overline{C}\ and\ P|)^2}{|C|*|P|*|\overline{C}|*|\overline{P}|}$
Cosine (IS)	$IS = \frac{|C\ and\ P|}{\sqrt{|C|*|P|}}$
Jmeasure (J)	$J = Pr(P) * [Pr(C|P)\log(\frac{Pr(C|P)}{Pr(C)})$ $+(1 - Pr(C|P))\log(\frac{1-Pr(C|P)}{1-Pr(C)})]$
J1measure ($J1$)	$J1 = Pr(P) * [Pr(C|P)\log(\frac{Pr(C|P)}{Pr(C)})]$
JFmeasure(JF)	$JF = \frac{(w1 \times J1 + w2 \times (\frac{Npu}{NT}))}{w1+w2}$
PiatetskyShapiro (PS)	$PS = \frac{|C\ and\ P|}{N} - \frac{|C|}{N} * \frac{|P|}{N}$

Table 5.1. *Some quality measures for association rules discovery*

As we can see, many quality measures have been proposed and one of the main questions is: which one to use?

5.2.3. *A mono- or a multi-objective problem?*

As many measures exist, some analyses of these measures have been proposed. For example, statistical studies (correlation analysis, principal component analysis, etc.) of these quality measures have been conducted. These analyses show that some of these measures are very correlated. For example, the study of Khabzaoui *et al.* exhibits five groups of measures, where each group is composed of correlated measures [KHA 04]. Within each group, only one measure should be chosen since using two measures from the same group will lead to the evaluation of the same aspect twice. In their study, Khabzaoui *et al.* proposed to choose the following measures: *support, confidence, interest, surprise* and *Jmeasure*.

Support (S): this is the most widely used measure of association rules. It measures rule frequency in the database by computing the percentage of transactions containing both the C part and the P part in the database.

Confidence (Conf): this measures the validity of a rule. It is the conditional probability of P given C.

Interest (I): this measures the dependency while privileging rare patterns in the region of weak support. It takes values in the interval $[0 , \infty[$:

– C and P are independent if the $interest$ equals to 1,

– the rule is interesting if the $interest$ is in the interval $]1, \infty[$.

surprise (R): this is used to measure the strenght of the affirmation. It enables us to search for surprising rules, that is to say rules that are not expected, since the number of times the rule is encountered do not belong to the measure. The *surprise* takes positive real values ($[0 , \infty[$).

Jmeasure: Smyth and Goodman [SMY 92] proposed the Jmeasure, which estimates the degree of interest of a rule and combines support and confidence. It is used in optimization as it allows us to evaluate in a single objective function both aspects of the rule; its frequency and its validity. During previous application of genetic algorithms to extract rules, some authors have observed that in the first generations of a genetic algorithm using the $Jmeasure$ as an evaluating function, the quality was often equal to zero. Therefore, Wang *et al.* [WAN 98] proposed another measure: the $J1measure$. However, the drawback of this formula is to cause a very low convergence of the algorithms. This is the reason why Araujo *et al.* [DEA 99] proposed the *JFmeasure*.

Using these five criteria, association rules may be evaluated in a complete way without privileging a specific criterion. This proposition leads to multi-objective models for the rule mining problem.

In the context of classification rules for imbalanced data in a medical application, Jacques *et al.* conducted another statistical analysis, leading to other results (as data is different and the context of classification rules is specific) [JAC 13b]. This shows that the models (and particularly the quality measures) used to deal with such association rules problems must be adapted to the context and to the specificities of data. It is then recommended to conduct a preliminary study to identify an efficient model.

In this section, we show that this rule mining problem can be seen as a combinatorial optimization problem. As the complexity is high and the number of possible rules is exponential, methods that are able to explore a huge search space are required. This is the reason why metaheuristics have been used for this purpose. The following section presents some of their uses and main characteristics.

5.3. Overview of metaheuristics for the association rules mining problem

Many metaheuristics, particularly evolutionary algorithms, have been applied to deal with association rules mining. Some recent reviews have been conducted on this subject. Readers may refer to the review of del Jesus *et al.* [JES 11] or the review of Mukhopadhyay *et al.*, dedicated to multi-objective approaches [MUK 14a].

5.3.1. *Generalities*

Metaheuristics are methods that explore efficiently the decision space composed of all the possible solutions. Hence the first question is to define what a solution to the problem is.

5.3.1.1. *Solution representation*

When mining rules, two designs are available: in *Michigan design*, each solution is a rule, while in *Pittsburgh design,* each solution is a set of rules (rule set). Pittsburgh design has a larger search space [BUR 07] and associated fitness function and operators are difficult to implement. However, in the Pittsburg design, there is no need to use a covering algorithm to encourage rules from the same solution (the set of rules) to cover different objects. In the Michigan design, without using any covering algorithm, several solutions (rules) can cover the same instances. In [BAC 07], Bacardit *et al.* compared Michigan and Pittsburgh representations. They concluded that both are suitable for data mining. The Michigan representation tends to overfit the data – rules are too specific – while the Pittsburgh one is sometimes too general and may miss some parts of the search space.

5.3.1.2. *Organization of the presentation of the methods*

As mentioned earlier, many quality measures have been proposed and several of them have to be jointly used to well characterize a rule. Hence most of the models proposed use several measures in either a mono- or a multi-objective approach. In mono-objective approaches, a linear aggregation of the measures is used. In multi-objective approaches, the Pareto dominance is exploited. Moreover, approaches may be different depending on the nature of data (categorical/numerical). Hence we choose to present methods according to the type of data they handle, rather than the mono- or multi-objective aspect. In the following sections, we first present metaheuristics dedicated to categorical data. Then, we study numerical data, with the specific case of fuzzy rules.

5.3.2. *Metaheuristics for categorical association rules*

Categorical association rules deal with either binary (boolean) or categorical (nominal) attributes. In a binary dataset, a rule of the form *IF (A and C and E) THEN (D and H)* means that if attributes A, C and E are present then attributes D and H are also present. the case of categorical data, where each attribute may have a finite number of values, each pair attribute-value is treated as a single attribute. This converts categorical data into binary data and allows us to deal with them using the same approaches. To describe metaheuristics developed to deal with such binary data, the most important components are presented.

5.3.2.1. *Rules encoding*

The encoding of a rule, independently of the fact that a *Pittsburgh* or a *Michigan* design is used, must indicate which are the attributes used in the condition part and which ones are in the consequent part. In a binary rule, each term represents the selection of one attribute. Two main types of representation have been used: either a binary encoding or an integer encoding.

– *Binary encoding* indicates for each attribute whether it belongs to the condition part, the consequent part or does not belong to the rules. Hence a $2k$ length chromosome is often used (if k represents the total number of attributes) and two bits are associated with each attribute [GHO 04, HU 07]. For example, a value 00 may indicate that the corresponding attribute belongs to the condition part, whereas the 11 value indicates that the attribute belongs to the consequent part. Other values (01 and 10) would indicate that the attribute does not belong to the rule. The rule *IF (A and C and E) THEN (D and H)* could be represented by: 00|01|00|11|00|01|10|11.

– *Integer encoding* lists the attributes that belong to the rule. For example, in ARMGA [YAN 09], and later in ARMMGA [QOD 11], an association rule of length n is represented by $n + 1$ integers. The first one is an indicator (also called *cut point*) that separates the condition part from the consequent one and the n other indicate the selected attributes. Hence the rule *IF (A and C and E) THEN (D and H)* would be represented by: $3|ACEDH$.

Using a binary encoding has the advantage that each rule has the same size, whereas with an integer encoding, the size of a rule depends on the number of attributes that belong to the rule. However, when the number of attributes in the data studied is very large (as it may happen in a Big Data environment), using a binary encoding may lead to very long chromosomes that are difficult to manipulate. The integer encoding reduces the length of the chromosome, which can be interesting. However, it does not reduce the search space as for each position in the chromosome, a large number of attributes are candidate. It should be noted that for categorical data, most of the time the dataset is first transformed into a binary one by considering each attribute-value pair as an attribute, but some authors proposed alternative ways to deal with such data. For example, Anand *et al.* proposed to use a two-part encoding for each attribute [ANA 09]. The first part is a binary encoding similar to the one for binary data indicating whether the attribute belongs or not to the rule, and the second part contains encoding for representing the M states of a categorical variable. Another example is given by Khabzaoui *et al.*, where an integer encoding is adapted to indicate at the same time the selected attribute and its associated value [KHA 04]. Such a rule could be represented as:

$$IF\ A = Val\_A_1\ and\ C = Val_{C3}\ THEN\ F = Val\_F_2.$$

5.3.2.2. *Objective function(s)*

As noted earlier, many quality measures have been proposed to evaluate the quality of rules. Support and confidence are the most commonly used, but many others have been used and combined to construct objective functions. Hence many models, mono- and multi-objective, have been proposed.

In addition to these classical quality measures, some authors introduced measures that are able to evaluate the interest of a rule and its usability.

For example, Ghosh *et al.* proposed to adopt a three-objective model based on *confidence*, *comprehensibility* and *interestingness* defined as follows [GHO 04]:

$$Comprehensibility\ (Comp) = \frac{log(1 + Nb\_Att(P))}{log(1 + Nb\_Att(C \cup P))}$$

where $Nb\_Att(P)$ and $Nb\_Att(C \cup P)$ indicate the number of attributes involved in the prediction part and in the whole rule, respectively. The minimization of this measure ensures a small number of attributes in the prediction part, which is more suitable to help the comprehensibility of the rule.

$$Interestingness\ (Int) = \frac{S(C \cup P)}{S(C)} \times \frac{S(C \cup P)}{S(P)} \times \frac{1 - S(C \cup P)}{N}$$

where S is the support measure defined in Table 5.1 and N is the total number of transactions. This measure is defined as the product of three probabilities: the probability of generating the rule given the condition part, the probability of generating the rule given the prediction part and the probability of not generating the rule given the whole dataset (1 minus the probability of generating the rule given the whole dataset). This set of three measures has also been used in Dehuri *et al.* [DEH 06].

Hu *et al.* also adopted a three-objective model using *confidence* (as described in Table 5.1) and *comprehensibility* defined above and the statistical correlation to substitute *support* [HU 07].

Similarly, for ARMGA, authors proposed to use the relative confidence as the interestingness measure, to ensure that the confidence of the rule is larger than the support (to discover positive association rules) [YAN 09]. It is defined as follows:

$$Relative\_Confidence(R\_Conf) = \frac{S(C \cup P) - S(C)S(P)}{S(C)(1 - S(P))}$$

where S is the support measure defined in Table 5.1.

5.3.2.3. *Operators*

Metaheuristics developed for the rule mining problem are mainly evolutionary approaches. Thus, we present here the proposed operators, particularly the crossover and mutation operators.

When binary encoding is used, classical operators may be adopted. For example, the one point or two-point crossovers may also be used as the bit-flip mutation [GHO 04, ANA 09]. Hu *et al.* proposed some other crossover operators, namely the Pareto neighborhood crossover, the combination operator and the annexing operator [HU 07].

When integer encoding is used, operators must be designed with care, as the variable length of chromosomes may lead to inconsistent rules. For example, duplicate attributes may appear or rules without any condition or prediction part may be constructed. Yan *et al.* chose a two-point crossover and applied nearest-neighbor substitution to ensure that any two genes in a chromosome are different [YAN 09]. This nearest-neighbor substitution is also used after the application of the exchange mutation. Such a mutation operator modifies the value of one of the integers of the chromosome. It may either change the separation of the *condition part* and the *prediction part* (if the first integer is modified) or change one attribute of the rule (and may generate duplicate attributes). On the other hand, Qodmanan *et al.* proposed to use the Order-1 crossover to avoid duplicate attributes [QOD 11]. Control is also realized when a mutation operator is applied.

In the case of categorical data, an operator may modify not only the selected attributes, but also its selected value for a given attribute belonging to the rule. Hence Khabzaoui *et al.* proposed two crossover operators depending on whether or not parent rules share a common attribute [KHA 08].

– *Crossover by value exchange:* if two rules X and Y have one or several common attribute(s) in their C parts, one common attribute is selected randomly. The value of the selected attribute in X is exchanged with its counterpart in Y.

– *Crossover by insertion:* conversely, if X and Y have no common attribute, one term is selected randomly in the C part of X and inserted in Y with a probability inversely proportional to the length of Y. The similar operation is performed to insert one term of Y in X.

In addition, four mutation operators are proposed and their probability of application is made in an adaptive manner:

– *value mutation* that replaces an attribute value by a randomly chosen one;

– *attribute mutation* that replaces a term by another. The value of the new attribute is randomly chosen in its domain;

– *insertion operator* that adds a term (a randomly chosen attribute with a randomly chosen value) in the rule;

– *delete operator* that removes a term of the rule, if possible.

5.3.2.4. *Algorithms*

When mono-objective approaches are adopted, using most of the time a compound fitness function based on some quality measures, classical genetic algorithms are used [YAN 09, QOD 11]. The performance of such algorithms is mostly linked to operators and specific reconstruction phase of solutions.

In the case of multi-objective approaches, standard and non-standard multi-objective evolutionary algorithms (MOEAs) have been used. For example, several works are based on the multi-objective NSGA-II algorithm, which are able to deal with several objectives, not only two and with the Pareto dominance concept [ANA 09, KHA 04]. Such multi-objective approaches have also been combined with exact approaches leading to hybrid metaheuristics [KHA 08] or developed in a parallel environment [KHA 05], to obtain better performances.

In a dynamic context, where transactions are updated during the search, some specific genetic algorithms have been proposed, such as dynamic mining of association rules using genetic algorithms (DMARG) and distributed and dynamic mining of association rules using genetic algorithms (DDMARG) [SHE 03, SHE 05].

5.3.3. *Evolutionary algorithms for quantitative association rules*

Quantitative association rules (also called numeric association rules) are not a simple extension of categorical rules as attributes have a continuous domain and may take an infinite number of different values. One way to deal with such numeric data could be to discretize them by partitioning the domain of each attribute into several intervals [YAN 09]. Then, algorithms for categorical data may be used. This can be a good solution if few attributes are numerical. However, when most of the attributes are numerical, it can be interesting to propose dedicated rule mining algorithms. In this context, such a rule may take the form:

$$IF\ (l_1 < term_1 < u_1)\ and\ (l_2 < term_2 < u_2)\ and\ ...(l_p < term_p < u_p)$$

$$THEN\ (l_{p+1} < term_{p+1} < u_{p+1})\ and\ ...(l_n < term_n < u_n)$$

where l_i represents a lower bound on $term_i$ and u_i an upper bound.

Therefore, specific encodings, fitness functions and operators have to be defined.

5.3.3.1. *Rules encoding*

In the context of numerical attributes, the encoding must indicate the lower and upper bounds of each attribute that belongs to the rule. As in categorical association rules, two main types of encoding have been proposed:

– *Binary-based encoding* indicates for each attribute whether it belongs to the condition part, the consequent part or does not belong to the rule; in addition, it indicates for attributes participating to the rule, their two bounds. In MODENAR algorithm, for example, the ith item is encoded in the ith decision variable and has three parts [ALA 08]. The first part can take three values : "0", "1" or "2", which indicate, respectively, that the item will be in the condition part, in the consequence part or not involved in the rule. This part is sometimes called the "type" of the attribute. The second and the third part of the decision variable represent the lower and upper bounds. A similar encoding is used in [MAR 11, MAR 14].

– *Integer-based encoding* indicates the list of attributes involved in the rule and, in addition, their associated intervals [ÁLV 12]. A special case is considered in the QuantMiner algorithm, where the list of attributes participating in the rule is fixed (given by the user) and the algorithm works on an optimal definition of intervals [SAL 07].

5.3.3.2. Objective function(s)

As for integer or categorical rule mining, many multi-objective approaches have been proposed, combining several quality criteria. For example, Alvares *et al.* proposed to use a linear aggregation of five measures as follows [ÁLV 12]:

$$Fitness = \alpha_S \times S + \alpha_C \times Conf + \alpha_{Nb} \times Nb\_Att +$$

$$\alpha_A \times Amplitude + \alpha_R \times ReCovering$$

where S is the support measure and $Conf$ the confidence measure defined in Table 5.1. Thus, they are able to adopt a mono-objective approach to look for the best rule regarding this fitness function.

QuantMiner, whose aim is to increase the quality of rules constructed on a fixed set of attributes, is based on the $Gain$ measure defined by [SAL 07]:

$$Gain = S(C \cup P) - MinConf \times S(C)$$

If the gain is positive, the amplitudes of the intervals are considered to favor those with small amplitudes.

Recently, Martin *et al.* proposed to use the *performance* measure, which is the result of the product of the support S and the measure CF, defined below [MAR 14]. According to them, this measure allows us to extract accurate rules with a good trade-off between local and general rules.

The measure CF for a rule $IF\ C\ THEN\ P$ is defined in three ways depending on whether Conf($C \to P$) is less than, greater than or equal to $S(P)$. $if\ Conf(C \to P) > S(P)$,

$$CF(C \to P) = \frac{Conf(C \to P) - S(P)}{1 - S(P)}$$

$if\ Conf(C \to P) < S(P)$,

$$CF(C \to P) = \frac{Conf(C \to P) - S(P)}{S(P)}$$

otherwise,

$$CF(C \to P) = 0$$

In their recent work, Martines *et al.* proposed a study of well-known quality measures for quantitative association rules, with respect to the weights of the measures that appear in a fitness function [MAR 16]. Therefore, several experiments have been carried out from 35 public datasets to show how the weights for confidence, support, amplitude and number of attributes measures included in the fitness function have an influence on different quality measures according to several minimum support thresholds.

5.3.3.3. *Operators*

Operators designed for categorical data can be used partially in the numerical case. However, intervals must also be managed. Thus, operators proposed in the literature mostly combine the two aspects (selection of the attributes involved in the rule and definition of their corresponding intervals).

When the binary-based encoding is used, every individual has the same length. Traditional operators may be used. For example, in Martin *et al.*, the crossover randomly interchanges the genes of the parents, while the mutation randomly modifies the interval of a selected attribute [MAR 14]. In their approach, Martinez *et al.* [MAR 11] distinguished two types of crossover, depending on whether attributes have the same type (the fact that an attribute belongs or not to the rule). If an attribute has the same type in the two parents, then the interval of the offspring is generated based on the parents one. On the contrary, if the attribute does not have the same type, then the type of the offspring is chosen randomly between the two parents. In the same manner, the mutation operator modifies either the type of an attribute or its interval.

When the integer-based encoding is used, chromosomes may have different lengths. Alvares *et al.* proposed to generate offsprings of the same length as parents [ÁLV 12]. An offspring is based on the same attributes as its parent and if a common attribute exists, the interval of the offspring is chosen randomly between the parents. As this crossover operator does not modify the chromosome deeply, they also proposed a mutation operator that, according to them, is more influential. The mutation proposed may alter one or several genes by modifying intervals associated with the attributes.

Let us note that modifying intervals may lead to inconsistent solutions if, for example, a lower bound becomes greater than an upper bound. Either operators prevent this effect or some repairing mechanisms are proposed.

5.3.3.4. *Algorithms*

As in categorical rule mining approaches, either mono-objective genetic algorithms using aggregation of several quality criteria or multi-objective approaches, based on the Pareto dominance property and the NSGA-II scheme, have been proposed. Nevertheless, two specific approaches dedicated to numerical data may be cited: MODEMAR and QuantMiner:

– *MODEMAR* (multi-objective differential evolution for mining numeric association rules) in which a Pareto-based multi-objective differential evolution algorithm is proposed as a search strategy for mining accurate and comprehensible numerical association rules [ALA 08]. The idea is to exploit the capacity of differential evolution algorithms to solve real-valued problems.

– *QuantMiner*, a genetic-based algorithm for mining quantitative association rules, that works directly on a set of rule templates (preset format of a quantitative association rule). This algorithm takes as an input, in addition to classical GA parameters, the minimum support and the minimum confidence and looks for the best intervals for the numerical attributes present in the rule templates [SAL 07].

5.3.4. *Metaheuristics for fuzzy association rules*

Approaches presented earlier were dedicated either to qualitative or quantitative data. However, the data in many real-world applications have a certain degree of imprecision that is not considered in the previous approaches, as they deal with sharp boundaries between intervals. Hence mining fuzzy association rules from quantitative data may solve some of the problems introduced by quantitative attributes. The use of fuzzy sets to describe associations between data allows us to extend the type of relationships that may be represented, to facilitate the interpretation of rules in linguistic terms and to avoid unnatural boundaries in the partitioning of attribute domains. Such an approach consists of transforming each quantitative value into a fuzzy set of linguistic terms (young/old, small/medium/large) using membership functions [PAL 12]. Explicitly, it is possible to define several fuzzy sets for $attribute_i$ with a membership function per fuzzy set. Degree of membership of each value of $attribute_i$ in any of the fuzzy sets specified for $attribute_i$ is based directly on the evaluation of the membership function of the particular fuzzy set with the value of $attribute_i$ as input [KAY 06]. It should be noted that some authors introduce the concept of fuzzy transaction as a fuzzy subset of items [DEL 03].

A fuzzy association rule is then expressed by

$$IF \ < attribute_1 \ is \ f_1 > \ and \ < attribute_2 \ is \ f_2 > \ and \ ...$$

$$< attribute_p \ is \ f_P >$$

$$THEN \ < attribute_{p+1} \ is \ g_{p+1} > \ and \ ... \ < attribute_n \ is \ g_n >$$

where f_i and g_i represent the fuzzy sets (associated with linguistic values) of the corresponding attributes.

As with categorical and quantitative data, adapted representation, objective functions and operators have to be defined. They are presented hereafter. However, the scope of this book is not to present all the fuzzy set theory; therefore, only the main principles are exposed here.

5.3.4.1. *Rules encoding*

As with categorical and quantitative data, a *Pittsburg* or a *Michigan* approach may be adopted. In this part, we focus on specificities linked to fuzzy rules. The encoding of a fuzzy rule must indicate attributes that belong to the rule (condition and consequent parts) and their associated linguistic values [MUK 14a]. Several encodings have been proposed:

– *Membership functions encoding* associates with each attribute the real-valued parameters of its corresponding (triangular) relationship function [KAY 05]. In fact, such a chromosome does not represent association rules, but only represents a suitable fuzzy clustering of the attribute domains. Later, the same authors introduce a second part to the chromosome, indicating which attribute is selected to belong to the rule [KAY 06]. With a similar idea, Acala-Fdez *et al.* [ALC 09b] proposed to use an $n \times m$ representation, (n attributes with m linguistic terms per attribute), in which the lateral displacements (symbolic translation) of the different linguistic terms are coded for each attribute. Then, a chromosome has the following form (where each gene is the displacement value of the corresponding linguistic term);

– *Direct encoding* combines two types of information. A binary encoding that indicates which attributes are selected to belong to the rule and a real encoding that associates with each attribute a real-value describing the fuzzy set. An example is given in [MAT 11], where temporal fuzzy association rules are studied. Such rules are encoded by:

$$C = (t_0, t_1, i_0, a_0, b_0, c_0, A_0, ..., i_k, a_k, b_k, c_k, A_k)$$

where the temporal interval is defined with t_0 and t_1 as integers. The attributes are integers denoted by i and the basic parameters of the triangular membership functions are real numbers indicated by a, b and c for association rules with k distinct attributes. A binary value in A_k determines whether this attribute belongs to the antecedent or the consequent part.

– *General encoding* associates with each attribute a quadruple of the form [FRE 13]:

$$< Attr_i \; Op_i \; Val_{ij} \; Selected_i >,$$

where:

– $Attr_i$ denotes th i^{th} attribute;

– Op_i denotes a comparison operator;

– Val_{ij} denotes the jth value of domain of;

– $Selected_i$ indicates whether the attribute is selected or not.

Let us note that this is a very general encoding that may be used for other types of data (an example has been given earlier for categorical data). The specificity here is that Val_{ij} can take a *linguistic value*.

5.3.4.2. *Objective function(s)*

Evaluating the goodness of a fuzzy rule requires the adaptation of classical rule discovery quality criteria. Therefore, several models have been proposed to define the *fuzzy support*, the *fuzzy confidence*, etc. [DEL 03]. For example, the *fuzzy support* may be the sum of the degrees of memberships of attributes belonging to the rule over all the transactions.

In their work, Kaya *et al.* [KAY 06] proposed to use *fuzzy support*, *average number of fuzzy sets* in the rule, maximum number of fuzzy sets and *fuzzy correlation* as objectives of a multi-objective problem for optimizing interesting fuzzy association rules. The *fuzzy correlation* is then defined as a correlation based on the *fuzzy support*.

Another multi-objective approach is adopted by Matthews *et al.* [MAT 11] to evaluate temporal fuzzy rules from quantitative data. They define the *temporal support*, the *temporal rule confidence*, the *fuzzy rule support* and the *membership function widths*. Using these four objectives, they choose to adopt a Pareto-based approach.

In their work, Acala-Fdez *et al.* [ALC 09b], proposed to combine several criteria in the fitness definition. Therefore, they define the fitness as the ratio between the *fuzzy support of the* 1-item set (item sets of cardinality 1) and the *suitability*.

5.3.4.3. *Operators*

The encodings used are mostly real encodings. Hence classical operators used for quantitative rules or more generally to real encoded solutions may be used here. For example, Acala-Fdez *et al.* [ALC 09b] used the Parent Centric BLX (PCBLX) operator defined in [LOZ 04] in the design of a real-coded memetic algorithm, whereas Kaya *et al.* [KAY 05, KAY 06] used the standard multi-point crossover operations.

5.3.4.4. *Algorithms*

Most of the approaches proposed to deal with fuzzy association rules mining are multi-objective ones. Hence several multi-objective evolutionary algorithms have been used, such as NSGA-II [MAT 11] or an adaptation of SPEA [KAY 05, KAY 06].

5.4. General table

Table 5.2 groups different metaheuristics proposed to deal with association rules mining. It allows us to compare the type of data, the encoding, operators and the optimization model (mono/multi-objective, objective functions, etc.) used. This shows the diversity of approaches, even if some common points may be observed, such as the need to use several objective functions to be able to well measure the quality of rules. Most of these approaches are evolutionary algorithms and use a Michigan-based representation.

Reference	Type data	Encoding	Operators	Objective function(s)	Mono/Multi	Algorithm
[HU 07]	Categorical	Binary (Michigan)	Pareto Neighborhood crossover, combining operator, annexing	Statistical correlation, Comprehensibility	Pareto	Pareto based co-evolutionary
[GHO 04]	Categorical	Binary (Michigan)	Multi-point crossover, Bit-flip mutation	Support, comprehensibility, interestingness	Pareto	MOGA
[ANA 09]	Categorical	Binary (Michigan)	Bit-flip mutation Crossover?	3 among: confidence, support comprehensibility, cosine, interestingness, Att_Freq	Pareto	NSGA-II
[GAN 14]	Binary	Ad-hoc		Supp, conf, interestingness, comprehensibility, lift, leverage conviction, coverage	Mono (aggregation)	PSO Firefly algorithm
ARMGA [YAN 09]	Categorical	Integer (Michigan)	Two-point crossover Exchange mutation	Relative_Confidence	Mono	GA
ARMMGA [QOD 11]	Categorical	Integer (Michigan)	Order-1-crossover Exchange mutation	Relative_Confidence	Mono	GA
[KHA 04] [KHA 05] [KHA 08]	Categorical	Integer based (Mich.) + value	Crossover by value mutation, Crossover by insertion, Mutation by value, Mutation by attribute	Support, confidence, Jmeasure, interest, surprise	Pareto	NSGA based Parallel NSGA based Exact + Evolutionnary
[MAR 11]	Quantitative Time series	Binary based (Michigan) + interval	Crossover by value exchange, Mutation of presence, Mutation of intervals	Support, confidence, Nb_At, amplitude, recovering	Mono (aggregation)	GA iterative scheme
MODENAR [ALA 08]	Quantitative	Binary based (Michigan) + interval	DE mutation DE crossover	Support, confidence, comprehensibility amplitude of intervals	Pareto (aggregation)	differential evolution (DE)
QAR-CIP-NSGA-II [MAR 14]	Quantitative	Binary based (Michigan) + interval	Uniform crossover Random mutation	Interestingness, comprehensibility, performance	Pareto	NSGA-II
[ALV 12]	Quantitative + Categorical	Integer based (Mich.) + interval	Uniform	Support, confidence, Nb_At, amplitude, recovering	Mono (aggregation)	GAR-plus
EARMGA [YAN 09]	Quantitative	Integer based (Michigan) + interval	Two-point crossover Exchange mutation	Relative_Confidence	Mono	GA
QuantMiner [SAL 07]	Quantitative	Integer based (fixed) + interval	Crossover by intervals exchange Mutation of intervals	Gain amplitude of intervals	Mono hierarchical	GA

Table 5.2. *Summary table of some metaheuristics for association rules*

Nevertheless, Djenouri *et al.* [DJE 12] propose to use a Bee Swarm optimization approach (BSO) for web association rule mining. Their fitness function is an aggregation of *confidence* and *support*. In the same idea, Ganghishetti *et al.* propose to solve the problem using a binary particle swarm optimization (BPSO), a binary firefly optimization and threshold accepting (BFFO-TA) and a binary particle swarm optimization and threshold accepting (BPSO-TA). A fitness function based on an aggregation of eight measures is used [GAN 14].

5.5. Conclusion

This chapter presents how metaheuristics can be used for association rules mining. According to the type of data (qualitative, quantitative and fussy), several encodings, objective functions and operators have been proposed. They have been briefly exposed in this chapter. A summary of some approaches has been given in the form of a summary table.

As we can see, many of the approaches are multi-objective ones and may lead to the construction of a Pareto front. In this case, one question is, how to select the final solution among all solutions of the front? When the Michigan type of encoding is used, which means that each solution encodes a single association rule, then the final solution may be the set of all of these non-dominated solutions. When the Pittsburg type of encoding is used, that is to say, a solution is a set of rules, then the choice of the final selected set must be realized.

Visualization representations can be used to facilitate the understanding and the comparison of rules. Classical representations deal with matrix-based representations where the two parts of the rule represent the two axes. For example, Ben Said *et al.* proposed to use a molecular representation to identify items belonging to the rule [BEN 13]. Based on this representation, they proposed a complete interface that allows us to interactively explore potential rules and visualized their performances. Such a visualization may help to select the final solution.

However, in the context of Big Data, where the number of features may be very large and the number of generated rules may also be huge, finding interesting visualization representations is beyond the scope of this book, but represents a great challenge.

6

Metaheuristics and (Supervised) Classification

One of the most important tasks in data mining is *supervised classification*. Such a task takes as input a collection of observations (or objects), each belonging to a small number of classes and described by its values for a fixed set of attributes (also called variables or features). The aim is to construct a classifier that can accurately predict the class to which a new observation belongs. Hence the aim of this data mining task is to build a model that predicts the value of the *class* from the known value of other variables. Classification has many applications. It can be used in:

– *fraud detection*, to determine whether a particular credit card transaction is fraudulent;

– *medical disease diagnosis*, to determine whether a patient may be infected by a disease in the future;

– *marketing*, to identify customers who may be interested in a given product;

– *social network analysis*, to predict useful properties of actors in a social network.

Supervised classification and mathematical optimization have strong links [CAR 13]. This chapter first provides a description of the classification task and a presentation of standard classification methods. Later, it discusses the use of metaheuristics to optimize those standard classification methods. Finally, it focuses on the use of metaheuristics for the classification rules discovery problem.

6.1. Task description and standard approaches

6.1.1. *Problem description*

As mentioned earlier, the aim of this data mining task is to build a model that predicts the value of one variable, called the "class", from the known values of other variables. The model is constructed using known observations, and then for new observations, the model is applied to determine the value of the target variable. Figure 6.1 illustrates this two-phase process.

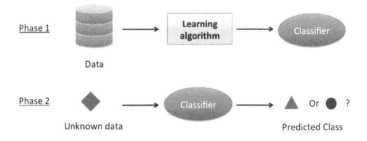

Figure 6.1. *Classification task*

In its basic form, the variable being predicted (the class) is categorical without any ranking. However, extensions have been proposed to consider cases where the class is described by a finite set of values with an ordering relation. Moreover, when the predicted variable is numerical, the task becomes a regression.

Several standard approaches have been proposed to deal with supervised classification. Let us remark that some of them, in particular the K-nearest neighbor, have no learning phase and simply give a way to affect a new observation to a class.

6.1.2. *K-nearest neighbor*

The K-nearest neighbor (K-NN) classification algorithm is one of the most fundamental and simple classification methods. It is suitable for a classification study when there is little or no prior knowledge about the distribution of the data. The K-nearest neighbor algorithm relies on the distance between observations in the feature space: a new observation is assigned to the most common class shared by the k nearest observations (its neighbors). Thus, the neighborhood is defined by the distance metric used. This distance metric should be carefully chosen. In the example of numerical attributes, the Euclidean distance is frequently used.

Figure 6.2 illustrates this method for several values of k. This example shows the lack of robustness, as according to the value chosen for k, the predicted class may be different – in the example of the figure, the class assigned is: Class 1, for $k = 3$; Class 2 for $k = 5$. It can then be used to weight the contribution of the neighbors, so that nearest neighbors contribute more to the average than more distant ones. If $k = 1$, then the observation is simply assigned to the class of its nearest neighbor.

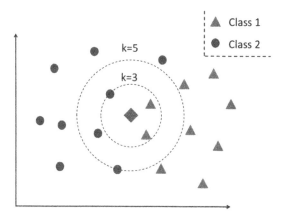

Figure 6.2. *K-nearest neighbor method*

6.1.3. *Decision trees*

Decision trees (or classification trees) are very popular for classification, since they are simple to understand and interpret. The tree building process is known as *binary recursive partitioning*. This process recursively splits (or "partitions") the observations into groups. At each iteration, the splitting operation is realized in a way that maximizes a score function. The score function is chosen so that it favors the degree to which each individual group contains observations that are all of the same class. Figure 6.3 shows an example of such a decision tree. In this example, the aim is to predict whether a patient has *flu* or not, according to some symptoms (which are the attributes of the dataset). We can observe that according to branches of the tree, different attributes are used.

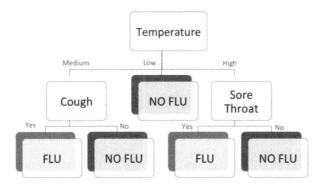

Figure 6.3. *Example of a decision tree to predict the flu*

The main difference between the different decision tree construction algorithms is the score function that is used to guide the splitting process. For example, the *Information gain* – used by the ID3, C4.5 [QUI 93] and C5.0 tree generation algorithms – is based on the concept of entropy used in information theory. The *Gini impurity* – used by the CART algorithm [BRE 84] – measures how often a randomly chosen observation from the dataset would be labeled incorrectly if it were randomly labeled according to the distribution of labels within the dataset.

6.1.4. *Naive Bayes*

The Naive Bayes classifier uses a probabilistic approach based on Bayes' theorem with strong (and naive) independence assumptions. To assign a class to an observation, it computes the conditional probabilities of the different classes, given the values of the features, and predicts the class with the highest conditional probability. Naive Bayes is simple and can be applied to multi-class classification problems, but it assumes independence between variables, which is typically untrue. In spite of this assumption, Naive Bayes classifiers often obtain good results in many complex real-world situations.

6.1.5. *Artificial neural networks*

Artificial neural networks (ANN) are widely used for supervised classification and are an alternative to other classification methods [ZHA 00]. An artificial neural network is a directed network of simple processors (called neurons) arranged in layers, with at least three layers. The first layer has input neurons, which send data via weighted links to the second layer of neurons; the nodes in the second layer (the hidden layer) perform a simple computation over the weighted input values that they receive and then send the results to the third layer, again via weighted links. The third layer usually consists of output neurons. The nodes in this output layer again perform a simple computation and the result of this computation becomes the output of the network. More complex systems will have more layers.

Here, Figure 6.4 describes a three-layer ANN and particularly a feed-forward multilayer perceptrons (MLPs), which is the most widely used model for addressing regression and classification problems. A new observation is presented to the MLP by describing it as a vector of input values fed to the input layer, and the resulting output of the MLP provides the class or predicted numerical value, in the case of regression.

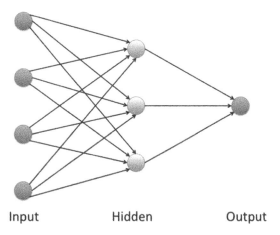

Input   Hidden   Output

Figure 6.4. *A three-layer artificial neural network*

6.1.6. *Support vector machines*

Support vector machines methods (SVMs), derived from statistical learning theory, classify points by assigning them to one of two disjoint half spaces [COR 95]. These half spaces are either in the original input space of the problem (for linear classifiers, see Figure 6.5) or in a higher dimensional feature space (for nonlinear classifiers). The assignment is realized by a kernel function. A keypoint of SVMs is the simultaneous minimization of the empirical classification error and the maximization of the geometric margin. Hence they are also known as maximum margin classifiers. SVMs generally produce very good results in term of class prediction accuracy, especially on small datasets. SVMs are widely used, as they have theoretical foundations, require only a dozen observations for training and are insensitive to the number of dimensions.

6.2. Optimization model

6.2.1. *A combinatorial problem*

While constructing a classifier, one of the questions is to identify attributes that participate to the model and to affect their values (separating values in decision trees, for example). Hence the classification task may be seen as a combinatorial problem. A feature selection step that is strongly linked to this task may be required. We do not consider it in this chapter, as it is the subject of the next one.

The description representation of solutions of the classification problem is linked directly to the way the classification model is expressed. Hence it is not possible here to give a general way to represent the solution. This point is discussed in the following section. On the contrary, whatever the classification model used, quality measures, which indicate the ability of the model to well classify new observations, are the same. They are described hereafter as well as the methodology of performance evaluation that is specific to this supervised data mining task.

6.2.2. *Quality measures*

Quality measures aim at evaluating the performance of a classifier. Regarding the application context, several aspects may have more or less importance. For example, the ability of correctly identifying positive observations may be more important (or not) than the ability to minimize misclassified observations. Hence several quality measures have been proposed in the literature. This part presents the most widely used ones.

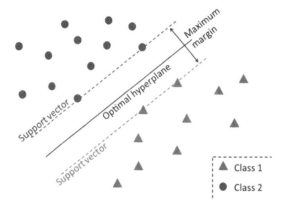

Figure 6.5. *Linear support vector machine*

6.2.2.1. *Confusion matrix*

A large number of quality measures are based on the confusion matrix. Table 6.1 presents such a matrix for a binary classification case (two classes). The two classes are often called *negative* and *positive*. The rows present the actual class of the test observations, whereas the columns present the class assigned (or predicted) by the classifier. The confusion matrix contains four characteristic values:

	Predicted	
	Negative	Positive
Actual Negative	TN	FP
Actual Positive	FN	TP

Table 6.1. *Confusion matrix*

TP and TN represent the number of observations from the test set that are correctly classified, whereas FN and FP represent the observations incorrectly classified; the error. Let us denote N as the total number of observations.

6.2.2.2. *Performance measures*

In their article, Salama *et al.* investigated several measures for learning decision tree algorithms [SAL 15]. Hence they provide a review of them. The following are the most widely used ones.

Accuracy measures the ratio of well-classified observations:

$$Accuracy = \frac{TP + TN}{N}$$

Error measures the ratio of misclassified observations:

$$Error = \frac{FP + FN}{N}$$

Precision measures the ratio of well-classified positive observations over all predicted positive observations:

$$Precision = \frac{TP}{TP + FP}$$

Sensitivity (or recall) measures the ratio of well-classified positive observations over all real positive observations:

$$Sensitivity = \frac{TP}{TP + FN}$$

Specificity measures the ratio of well-classified negative observations over all real negative observations:

$$Specificity = \frac{TN}{TN + FP}$$

Jaccard coefficient measures the ratio of well-classified positive observations over all the observations neglecting the true negative:

$$Jaccard = \frac{TP}{TP + FP + FN}$$

M-estimate is a parametric function of parameter m:

$$M\text{-}estimate = \frac{TP + m.\frac{TP}{N}}{TP + FP + m}$$

Designing supervised learning systems mostly requires finding the appropriate trade-offs between several quality measures, for example between model complexity and accuracy or sensitivity and specificity. Therefore, some combined measures have been proposed to take into account several aspects within a single performance measure.

F-measure computes a harmonic mean between *precision* and *recall*:

$$F\text{-}measure = \frac{2 \times Precision \times Recall}{Precision + Recall}$$

Product of sensitivity specificity:

$$Sensitivity \times Specificity = \frac{TP}{TP + FN} \times \frac{TN}{TN + FP}$$

The choice of the quality measure is highly correlated with the application context and may be considered as the objective function by an optimization method used to deal with classification. Moreover, as this problem is, in general, a multi-objective optimization problem, several multi-objective approaches have been proposed.

6.2.3. *Methodology of performance evaluation in supervised classification*

Data mining models constructed by algorithms must be evaluated with regard to their utility, which is linked directly to their generality that may be summarized by this question: can the proposed model be used on new data, not used for its construction? Classifiers are computed thanks to observations for which the class is known. The aim is then to classify unknown observations. However, to test the performance of a classifier, it is applied on observations for which the class is known (without considering the information about the class) and a comparison is done between the effective class and the predicted one. To ensure that observations used to evaluate performance have not been exploited during the classifier construction process, a separation between training data and validation data is realized, as illustrated in Figure 6.6 and a cross-validation is applied [REF 09, LAR 14].

Cross-validation is a technique that ensures that models constructed are generalizable to an independent, unknown dataset. The most common methods are two-fold cross-validation and, more generally, the k-fold cross-validation. In the first case, data are split randomly into a *training dataset* and a *validation dataset* (or test dataset) of the same size or representing two-thirds and one-third of the initial data, respectively. The training dataset is used to construct the model, whereas the validation dataset is used to evaluate the model (by comparing, for example in a classification task, predictions of the model to real classes). In a k-fold cross-validation, data are split into k independent and subsets of equal size ($k = 10$ is a widely used value, see Figure 6.7). The model is constructed using data from $k - 1$ subsets and evaluated on the remaining one. This is done iteratively, such that k models are constructed and evaluated. The overall performance of the method is computed using the k evaluations. The leave-one-out cross validation (LOOCV) refers to the case in which k equals the number of instances. The choice between a two-fold cross-validation and a k-fold cross-validation may depend on the size of the dataset. For large datasets, including a large number of instances, the two-fold validation can be used; however, when the number of instances is limited, it is preferable to use the k-fold cross-validation.

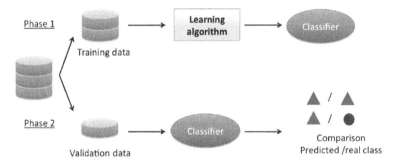

Figure 6.6. *Performance evaluation methodology in supervised classification*

6.3. Metaheuristics to build standard classifiers

6.3.1. *Optimization of* K-NN

A drawback of *K-NN* is its sensitivity to the k parameter (see Figure 6.2 for an illustrative example). In their work, Marinakis *et al.* proposed several metaheuristics (Tabu Search, genetic algorithm and ant colony) for the feature selection problem in classification (for the modelization of such a problem, see Chapter 7). As they use the *K-NN* algorithm for the classification step (and particularly the $1 - NN$ version), they proposed dynamic approaches based on a genetic algorithm (*Gen-knn* and the corresponding weighted version *Gen-wknn*), in which the value of k is changed dynamically depending on the number of generations [MAR 08]. The idea is to ensure diversity of the individuals in each generation. Their main objective is to optimize the *accuracy*.

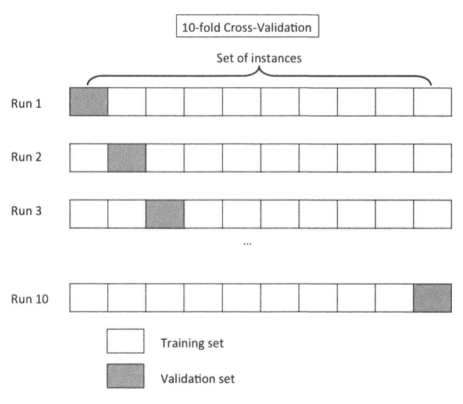

Figure 6.7. *Cross validation (example of a 10-fold)*

6.3.2. *Decision tree*

Top-down induction of decision trees (TDIDT) is the most common approach in the literature for learning decision trees and employs a divide-and-conquer approach. Nonetheless, the divide-and-conquer approach represents a deterministic, greedy search strategy to create a decision tree; the selection of the best attribute is made locally at each iteration, without taking into consideration its influence over the subsequent iterations. This makes the algorithm vulnerable to local optima traps [SAL 15]. Hence metaheuristics have been proposed to explore the huge search space composed by all possible decision trees.

For example, the HEAD-DT (Hyper-Heuristic Evolutionary Algorithm for Automatically Designing Decision-Tree) algorithm makes use of a regular generational single-objective evolutionary algorithm, in which individuals are collections of building blocks of top-down decision tree induction algorithms [BAR 12]. Typical operators from evolutionary computation are employed, such as tournament selection, mutually exclusive genetic operators – reproduction, crossover and mutation – and a typical stopping criterion that halts evolution after a predefined number of generations. The encoding of individuals in HEAD-DT is in the form of integer vectors to represent a large set of tree constructive strategies. Each gene takes a value in a predefined range, which is later mapped into specific procedures/functions within the top-down greedy approach of decision tree induction. The set of genes is divided into four categories:

– *split genes* that represent the design component that is responsible for selecting the attribute to split the data in the current node of the decision tree;

– *stopping criteria genes* that select among five different strategies for stopping the tree growth;

– *missing value genes* that represent missing value strategies in different moments of the induction/deduction process;

– *pruning genes* that index one of five well-known approaches for pruning a decision tree and also the option of not pruning at all.

The objective function used is the *F-Measure*, which is a predictive performance measure that indicates a trade-off between precision and recall and is suitable for both balanced and imbalanced data. They evaluate their algorithm in two contexts: i) evolution of a decision tree algorithm tailored to one specific dataset at a time (specific framework); ii) evolution of a decision tree induction algorithm from multiple datasets (general framework). One of the drawbacks of this algorithm is the complexity of the trees generated. Hence a bi-objective version has also been proposed: the MOHEAD-DT

(Multi-Objective Hyper-Heuristic Evolutionary Algorithm for Automatically Designing Decision-Tree) algorithm [BAS 15]. It considers the two objectives: i) F-Measure as mentioned earlier; ii) number of nodes in the tree, which is a suitable estimation of model complexity for decision trees. They compare two multi-objective approaches, namely the lexicographic approach and the Pareto approach, and show that in their experiments, the lexicographic approach manages to find very efficient solutions.

Ant colony optimization (ACO) algorithms have also been proposed to deal with the decision tree construction.

For example, *ant-tree-miner* is an ACO-based algorithm for inducing decision trees [OTE 12]. It follows the traditional divide-and-conquer approach, with the difference that an ACO procedure is used during the tree construction to select the nodes (attributes) of the tree. Instead of applying a greedy deterministic selection, ant-tree-miner uses a stochastic process based on heuristic information and pheromone values. To create a candidate decision tree, an ant starts by selecting an attribute from the construction graph. The probability of selecting an attribute is based on both their heuristic function (inspired from C4.5 algorithm) value and the pheromone amount. Once an attribute is selected to represent a decision node, branches corresponding to each attribute condition are created.

An extension has been recently proposed in *ant-tree-miner$_M$* for learning an extended multi-tree classification model, which consists of multiple decision trees, one for each class value [SAL 14]. As one of the most important aspects of the ACO algorithm is the choice of the quality measure used to evaluate a candidate solution to update pheromone, Salama *et al.* explore, in their recent paper, the use of various classification quality measures for evaluating the candidate multi-tree models constructed by the ants during the execution of the ant-tree-miner_M algorithm [SAL 15].

Another example of the ACO algorithm proposed to construct decision trees is given by ACDT (Ant Colony Algorithm for constructing Decision Trees) proposed by Boryczka *et al.* [BOR 10]. In ACDT, each ant chooses the appropriate attribute for splitting in each node of the constructed decision tree according to the heuristic function and pheromone values. The heuristic function is based on the Twoing criterion (similarly to CART algorithm), which helps ants to divide the observations into two groups, connected with the analyzed attribute values. Pheromone values represent the best way (connection) from the superior to the subordinate nodes – all possible combinations in the analyzed subtrees. The objective function is a weighted sum of the tree size (the number of nodes) and the accuracy. Experiments show that this algorithm manages to produce high quality trees, but of larger size, compared to CART or ant-tree-miner, for example. More recently, some improvements have been proposed to enhance the effectiveness of Ant Colony Decision Tree algorithms by co-learning [BOR 15]. It should be noted that this article also provides an interesting review of literature on ACO for classification.

Besides decision trees, *random forest* is another approach proposed for classification. It operates by constructing a multitude of decision trees at training time and outputting the class that is the mode of the classes of the individual trees. Random decision forests correct for decision trees' habit of overfitting to their training set. In this context, Bursa *et al.* proposed an hybrid method combining ant colony metaheuristics and evolutionary computing technique to generate trees. This method benefits from both the stochastic process and the population approach, which allows the algorithm to evolve more efficiently than each method alone [BUR 07].

6.3.3. *Optimization of* ANN

Optimization of *ANNs* may deal with several aspects. It may either concern the topology optimization of multi-layer neural networks or the training of the neural network. Metaheuristics have been proposed to deal with these two aspects.

For example, in [IGE 05], three applications of evolutionary optimization of neural systems are presented: topology optimization of multi-layer neural networks for face detection, weight optimization of recurrent networks for solving reinforcement learning tasks and hyperparameter tuning of support vector machines (see section 6.3.4). In their work, they put emphasis on strategy adaptation, a feature of evolutionary methods that allows for the control of the search strategy during the optimization process.

Several *particle swarm optimization* (PSO) approaches have been proposed to deal with optimization of ANN. For example, the radial basis function neural network (RBFNN, an alternative to multilayer perceptrons) using PSO is proposed. As the controlling parameter of kernel function is an important parameter of RBFNN, the particle swarm optimization is used to choose suitable controlling parameters [HUA 08]. However, the conventional PSO suffers from being stapled in local optimum and the results for optimizing controlling parameters of RBFNN should be improved further and leads to the proposition of an hybrid approach [LEU 12]. Here, a PSO with automatic linearly decreased inertia weight is proposed to improve the performance of PSO. In addition, an automatic control method for inertia weight is introduced to set the inertia weight of each particle, which can improve the convergence speed. A global and local search technique is also employed to further refine the solution.

In [GRE 12], the training of neural networks (NN) is addressed. The metaheuristic *central force optimization* (CFO) and PSO are compared. CFO is a recent optimization metaheuristic that has been proposed and developed by Formato [FOR 07]. Although other algorithms use genes, particles, ants or they like to mimic natural behavior, CFO uses probes as its basic population. These probes are scattered throughout the search space and as time progresses, they slowly move towards the probe that has achieved the highest mass or fitness. This movement of the probes is built upon the mathematical concepts that have been developed to describe the force between two observations. In their study, both approaches (CFO and PSO) use a representation that depicts the weights between neurons in the given NN and it is assumed that all biases are zero. The objective function is mean square error (MSE), which computes the difference between the expected output and the actual output. The experiments shows that CFO manages to obtain good results even if it does not outperform PSO.

As metaheuristics show an efficient ability to train neural networks, some authors propose a comparison between several approaches [KHA 12]. Hence two gradient descent algorithms, namely back propagation and Levenber-Marquardt, and three population-based heuristics, namely bat algorithm (a recent population-based metaheuristic approach based on hunting behavior of bats), genetic algorithm and particle swarm optimization, are compared. Their conclusions on their benchmarks establish the advantages of their new metaheuristic, the bat algorithm, over the other algorithms in the context of e-learning.

This last work shows the interest of the metaheuristic community to address this problem. According to the benchmarks, and the type of neural network, some or other metaheuristics may outperform the other, but what is important is their ability to well explore the large search space composed of all configurations of neural networks.

6.3.4. *Optimization of* SVM

Although the SVM learning algorithm generally has a good performance and robust statistical foundation, the quality of an SVM classifier is largely influenced by the parameters of kernel functions. The kernel function parameters, together with the regularization parameter, are the *hyperparameters* of the SVM. In practice, the standard method to determine the hyperparameters is grid-search. In simple grid-search, the hyperparameters are varied with a fixed step-size through a wide range of values and the performance of every combination is measured. Because of its computational complexity, grid-search is only suitable for the adjustment of very few parameters. Perhaps the most elaborate systematic techniques for choosing multiple hyperparameters are gradient descent methods. However, these approaches have some significant drawbacks. The kernel function has to be differentiable. The score function for assessing the performance of the hyperparameters also has to be differentiable with respect to kernel and regularization parameters. This excludes reasonable measures such as the number of support vectors. Hence optimization approaches have been proposed to deal with SVM model selection (hyperparameter selection) and particularly evolutionary approaches.

In [FRI 05], Friedrichs *et al.* proposed an evolutionary approach to determine multiple SVM hyperparameters: covariance matrix adaptation evolution strategy (CMA-ES). It is used to determine the kernel from a parameterized kernel space and to control the regularization. They conclude that CMA evolution strategy is a powerful, general method for SVM hyperparameter selection. It can handle a large number of kernel parameters and requires neither differentiable kernels and model selection criteria nor separability of the data. Following this study, in [SUT 06], a three-objective approach is proposed to take into account several aspects of the optimization. It is based on the minimization of the false positive rate, the false negative rate and the number of support vectors to reduce the computational complexity.

In [SHA 13], a less conventional metaheuristic is used to optimize the parameters of SVM: the firefly algorithm (FFA). A firefly is an insect that glows by the process of bioluminescence. For this algorithm, some idealized rules are followed: i) one firefly is attracted to every other firefly irrespective of their sex; that is, attraction is purely on the basis of the brightness of the fireflies; ii) the more the brightness between the two fireflies, the more is the attraction between the two. In case there is no brighter firefly, the movement occurs randomly; iii) how bright a firefly is, is determined by its value of the objective function. To optimize SVM parameters, each firefly represents a parameter set and the movement to other firefly in the swarm modifies the parameter values.

As metaheuristics may require a large number of evaluations (each of them requires a SVM execution), it may be useful to utilize parallelism to reduce the time needed for search. Hence Runarsson *et al.* proposed the application of a parallel evolutionary strategy (ES) to model selection for support vector machines [RUN 04]. In this work, an asynchronous parallel evolution strategy is chosen because the load on the processors is usually unbalanced.

In a context of predictive modeling of hospital readmissions, Zheng *et al.* proposed various data mining approaches to identify the risk group of a particular patient, including neural network model, random forest (RF) algorithm and a hybrid model of swarm intelligence heuristic and support vector machine (SVM) [ZHE 15]. The particle swarm optimization (PSO) is implemented for the parameter search to build an optimal SVM classifier based on a radial basis function (RBF) for the kernel. In this study, the position represents the spread of the RBF in SVM. The proposed neural network algorithm, the RF and the SVM classifiers are used to model patients' characteristics, such as their age, insurance payer, medication risk, etc. Experiments are conducted to compare the performance of the proposed models. Experimental results indicate that the proposed prediction SVM model with particle swarm parameter tuning outperforms other algorithms.

A recent study suggests that a less complex optimization technique, such as a random search (RS), may be sufficient for SVM hyperparameter optimization [MAN 15]. The experiments used a large number of datasets from UCI repository, mostly of low dimensionality, and compared RS with three metaheuristics commonly used for SVM hyperparameter tuning, namely GA, PSO and estimation of distribution algorithms (EDA), and with another optimization technique, the initial grid search (GS). It was concluded that according to the tests, all the tuning techniques found better hyperparameter values than the default values used for SVM. However, none of these techniques show better performance in general; hence using a simple technique may be, in some case, a good compromise.

6.4. Metaheuristics for classification rules

Classification rules are another way to express classifier models. The objective of a rule-based classification system is to identify a good set of classification rules that can efficiently represent the training set and well classify new observations. A classification rule can be expressed as an *if-then* rule of the form $C \Rightarrow Class$ (or *IF C THEN Class*), where C is the condition part (antecedent) and $Class$ the prediction part (class to predict). It is then very similar to association rules of the form *IF C THEN P*, the difference being that in classification rules, a single prediction has to be addressed: the class to predict.

Hence this part does not repeat all the elements that have been described for association rules and the reader interested in classification rules, should first read the chapter on association rules. This part presents specificities of classification rules regarding association rules.

6.4.1. *Modeling*

As for association rules, two representations of solutions have been proposed: the *Michigan design*, in which each solution is a rule, and the *Pittsburgh design,* in which each solution is a set of rules (rule set). From the classification point of view, the *Pittsburgh* design is more useful, since each solution represents a complete classifier system [MUK 14b]. The number of rules encoded in a solution can either be fixed or variable.

The rules' encoding depends on the type of attribute of the dataset (categorical, numerical, etc.) as for association rules. Numerical data must be handled with care and discretization methods are often used [VAN 15]. However, an important point is the type of the *Class* attribute. If this attribute is continuous, it must be first discretized to make it categorical and used in the prediction part of the rule. It must be noted that many metaheuristic approaches are focused on evolving fuzzy classification rules that allow us to indicate the degree of membership to a given class. Thus, the representation may consist of a direct encoding, in which a solution encodes a set of rules by describing for each attribute the corresponding fuzzy set parameters for each rule [PUL 08]. To reduce the search space, a mixed encoding (integer and real value) may be proposed. The integer values represent the selected rules and the real values encode the parameters of the fuzzy sets [ANT 12].

6.4.2. *Objective function(s)*

As the aim is to find rules, some of the objective functions used to optimize association rules (support, confidence, coverage, etc.) may also be used for classification rules. However, in a supervised context, it is often more interesting to use performance measure of classifiers (such as accuracy, sensibility, sensitivity, etc.). In addition, for association rules, those measures may be conflicting and complementary. Thus, multi-objective approaches are often proposed.

A special case should be considered with care: *imbalanced data* in which the proportion of positive and negative observations (in a binary classification problem) is unequal. Indeed, usually, the accuracy of a classifier is evaluated in terms of percentage of correct classifications and the objective of a classifier identification process is to maximize this percentage (or equivalently to minimize the misclassification rate). This objective might not be appropriate for application domains characterized by highly imbalanced distributions of patterns, with positive observations comprising just a small fraction of the available data used to train the classifier or when the cost of misclassification of the positive patterns is different from the cost of misclassification of the negative patterns. In this example of unbalanced data, Pappa and Freitas recommend to use sensitivity $\times$ specificity as the fitness function (in their protein data, only 6.04% of observations have the positive class) [PAP 09].

Following this recommendation, in the context of fuzzy classification rules, Ducange *et al.* adopted a three-objective approach that aims at reducing complexity while improving specificity and sensitivity [DUC 10]. Another recommendation is to use the receiver operating characteristic (ROC) curve analysis that has proved to be very effective to compare different binary classifiers. In a ROC curve, the true positive rate (sensitivity) is plotted as a function of the false positive rate (1-specificity) for different cut-off points (see Figure 6.8). Each point on the ROC curve represents a sensitivity/specificity pair corresponding to a particular decision threshold. A classifier with perfect discrimination has a ROC curve that passes through the upper left corner (100% sensitivity and 100% specificity). Therefore, the closer the ROC curve is to the upper left corner, the higher the overall accuracy of the classifier.

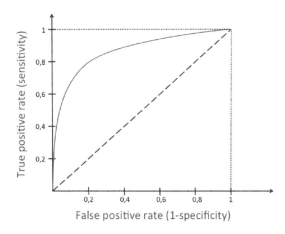

Figure 6.8. *Receiver operating characteristic (ROC) curve*

Imbalanced data represents a great challenge, particularly if a minority class is of particular interest. This problem may be addressed using partial classification techniques. The task of partial classification (also known as nugget discovery) aims at finding patterns that represent a strong description of a specified class (even if this class has few representative observations in the data) [IGL 05]. This may be the case while studying data from a hospital and trying to identify factors that may predict one or the other disease that may appear in only a few percents of the whole hospital patients. Patterns discovered by partial classification are, therefore, individual descriptions of the class under study. Figure 6.9 shows, in a partial classification context, relationships between observations that verify the condition part of the rule and/or the class to explain. Regarding the context, it may be more interesting to optimize the support of the rule (which is represented by the intersection), the confidence of the rule (intersection/condition) or the coverage (intersection/class). According to De la Iglesia *et al.*, strong rules may be defined as those that meet certain confidence and coverage thresholds, which leads to the definition of the *cc-optimal subset* (coverage-confidence optimal subset) of rules that is composed by rules that are optimal with respect to coverage and confidence [IGL 06]. Then, a bi-objective approach considering the two objective functions *confidence* and *coverage* is proposed.

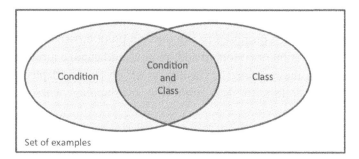

Figure 6.9. *Venn diagram illustrating repartition of observations [IGL 06]*

In a similar context of partial classification, Jacques *et al.* proposed to adopt a three-objective approach, considering also the *confidence* and the *sensitivity* (which is equivalent to the coverage in a partial classification context) in addition to the *minimization of the number of terms* of the rules to obtain simpler rule sets [JAC 13b].

6.4.3. *Operators*

Operators are not very different from those used in association rules. The difference is mainly due to the fact that the prediction part may not be changed, as it is fixed to the class here.

When fixed length solution encodings or binary encodings are used, standard uniform crossover (1- or 2-point(s) crossovers) and bit-flip mutation are used. This bit-flip mutation may use a biased mutation probability when the number of 0 and 1 expected is not equal. When a very large number of attributes are selected to participate in a rule, only a few of them are accepted. Hence a larger probability is assigned to the mutation from 1 to 0, than that from 0 to 1. Otherwise, too many attributes will be selected [MUK 14b].

For real-values encoding, simulated binary crossover (SBX) and standard polynomial mutation operators are mostly employed. Parents are mainly selected using fitness proportionate selection, as stochastic universal sampling (SUS) or roulette wheel. Less frequently, elite selection and tournament are used.

In the case of a Pittsburgh design, rule sets have to be modified. In this context, Ducange *et al.* proposed to use the one-point crossover operator and three kinds of mutation operators to add, remove and change a rule of the rule set [DUC 10]. In their approach, Casillas *et al.* proposed adapted crossover and mutation operators to deal with rule overlapping when using rule sets [CAS 09].

For local search approaches, the neighborhood is defined by applying neighbor operators. For example, Jacques *et al.* define the neighborhood of a given rule set by adding/removing or modifying one term to one of the rule [JAC 13b].

6.4.4. *Algorithms*

Since (supervised) classification is a very challenging task in many application domains, different authors propose to address this problem through different approaches. As explained in the objective function section, many of them are multi-objective approaches to deal with the several aspects of expected quality of rules. Hence several multi-objective evolutionary algorithms have been proposed. A variety of approaches may be found: particle swarm optimization algorithms, ant colony optimization algorithms, simulated annealing or multi-objective local search approaches.

With regard to MOEA, De la Iglesia *et al.* proposed to adopt a multi-objective metaheuristic, based on a NSGA-II scheme, to produce a set of cc-optimal rules (coverage-confidence optimal rules). To avoid the construction of very similar rules, they explore the concept of rule similarity and experiment with a number of modifications of the crowding distance, to increase the diversity of the partial classification rules. Hence the whole method includes multi-objective metaheuristics to induce the rules, measures of rule dissimilarity to encourage the production of dissimilar rules, and rule clustering algorithms to evaluate the results obtained [IGL 05, IGL 06].

In their work, Holden and Freitas propose a hybrid particle swarm optimization/ant colony optimization (PSO/ACO) algorithm. Unlike a conventional PSO algorithm, this hybrid algorithm can cope with nominal attributes directly, without converting nominal values into binary numbers in a preprocessing phase [HOL 05]. A second version (PSO/ACO2) is proposed in [HOL 08] to directly deal with both continuous and nominal attribute values. Their experiments on 27 public-domain, real-world datasets that are often used to benchmark the performance of classification algorithms show that the PSO/ACO2 algorithm is competitive in terms of accuracy and that it may produce simple rule sets.

Recently, a novel chemistry-based metaheuristic optimization method for mining of classification rules has been proposed [ALA 12]. This approach, named artificial chemical reaction optimization algorithm (ACROA) works as follows: Encoding of the reactants for ACROA depends on the problem under interest. In the classification rule problem, a reactant is composed of n atoms (the number of attributes) and each atom has two fields (a flag and a value). ACROA begins with a set of uniform initial reactants in a solution. Reaction rules (similar to chemical reactions) define the interaction among one or two reactants, which may lead to the production of a new reactant. Thus, reactants are consumed and produced via chemical reactions. The algorithm ends when the termination criterion is met similar to the state when no more reactions can take place (inert solution). In their approach, a weighted sum of comprehensibility and predictive accuracy is used as the objective function. This algorithm has not been widely tested for the moment, but it illustrates the keen interest of the metaheuristic community for the classification problem.

In parallel to population-based approaches, some local search approaches have been proposed.

In their work, Mahamadi *et al.* adopt a simulated annealing metaheuristic for constructing a fuzzy classification system: simulated annealing based fuzzy classification system (SAFCS) [MOH 08]. A solution represents a set of fuzzy rules. The quality of a fuzzy rule is evaluated by the number of correctly classified observations and the fitness function of a rule set is to minimize the number of misclassified observations. Then, a standard simulated annealing is used. It appears on the benchmarks used for experiments that this approach allows us to obtain quite good results.

Another approach has been proposed by Jacques *et al.* to deal with the classification rule problem through a three-objective approach (maximize confidence, maximize sensitivity and minimize number of terms) [JAC 13b, JAC 15]. The dominance-based local search (DMLS) approach is an adaptation of single-objective local search algorithms (such as Hill Climbing) to multi-objective problems. This approach uses a dominance relation, like Pareto dominance, to handle each objective separately. Thus, the main difference for a single-objective approach is that DMLS has to cope with a population of compromise solutions, instead of one single solution. Several solution selection strategies, as well as neighborhood exploration strategies, have been studied and compared to the single-objective version of the method. It appears that the multi-objective version allows better solutions to be obtained than with the single-objective version.

Classification rules are a very flexible way to express classifiers. Moreover, they are easy to understand. This explains that they are widely used in different communities (for example, in medicine). Regarding the high combinatoric (due to the large number of combinations "attributes-values" that may constitute a rule) and the existence of quality measures that may participate in the definition of an objective function, classification rules problem is a very good candidate for metaheuristic approaches. This explains the variety of methods proposed.

6.5. Conclusion

Supervised classification has been widely used in the literature and the metaheuristic community contributes to the proposition of interesting models and approaches.

In a Big Data context, such metaheuristics have several advantages that not only deal with the potentially large size of datasets. As metaheuristics are very flexible, they can be adapted, through the representation they use, to the variety of data and then may be used to simultaneously deal with different types of attribute. Moreover, in a dynamic environment, when new observations regularly complete the dataset or when the significance of attributes changes over the time, metaheuristics can used previously obtained classifiers to make them evolved and then keep some stability on classifiers over time. This is an important fact for decision makers that will use these classifiers.

Let us remark that in some applications, the amount of features (attributes) is large and the performance of the classifier may be penalized, as manipulating all these features can be time consuming, and all the features are not necessarily significant for the classification task. In this example, a feature selection has to be realized to improve the performance of the classifier. It will be the subject of the next chapter.

7

On the Use of Metaheuristics for Feature Selection in Classification

In practice and particularly in the case of Big Data, data miners are confronted with a large number of variables (or features) and often too many, that make them impossible to use conventional algorithms. For example, in classification, all the variables that are stored in the database are not all necessary for accurate discrimination. Including them in the classification model can even reduce the performance of the model. Feature selection, also known as variable selection, attribute selection or variable subset selection, aims at selecting an optimum relevant set of features or attributes that are necessary for classification. An appropriate feature selection can enhance the effectiveness of an inference model. In [LIU 07], Liu and Motoda indicate that the effects of feature selection are as follows: 1) to improve performance (speed of learning, predictive accuracy or simplicity of rules); 2) to visualize the data for model selection; 3) to reduce dimensionality and remove noise. In this chapter, we propose to show how feature selection can be realized with metaheuristics and why metaheuristics can help realize the feature selection task in a Big Data context.

We first give a general description of the feature selection problem. In section 7.2, the feature selection problem is modeled as an optimization problem and elements for solving it through metaheuristics are discussed. A general overview of metaheuristics for feature selection is then given.

7.1. Task description

There are three classical approaches to realize feature selection in classification: filter approach, wrapper approach and embedded approach [GUY 03, KOH 97].

7.1.1. *Filter models*

Relying on the characteristics of data, filter models evaluate features without using any classification algorithms [KIR 92] (see Figure 7.1). A typical filter algorithm consists of two steps. In the first step, it ranks features based on certain criteria. Feature evaluation could be either univariate or multivariate. In the univariate scheme, each feature is ranked independently of the feature space, while the multivariate scheme evaluates features in a batch way. Therefore, the multivariate scheme is naturally capable of handling redundant features.

The two phases of the filter method according to [LIU 07] are:

1) feature selection using measures such as information, distance, dependence or consistency; no classifier is engaged in this phase;

2) a classifier is learned on the training data with the selected features and tested on the test data.

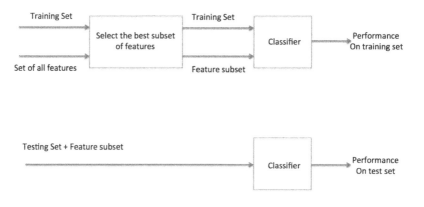

Figure 7.1. *Filter model for feature selection: learned on the training set and tested on the test dataset*

7.1.2. *Wrapper models*

Filter models select features independent of any specific classifiers. However, the major disadvantage of the filter approach is that it totally ignores the effects of the selected feature subset on the performance of the classifier. The optimal feature subset should depend on the specific biases and heuristics of the induction algorithm. Based on this assumption, wrapper models utilize a specific classifier to evaluate the quality of selected features and offer a simple and powerful way to address the problem of feature selection, regardless of the chosen learning machine [KOH 97]. A wrapper model consists of two phases:

– phase 1: feature subset selection, which selects the best subset using the accuracy of the classifier (on the training data) as a criterion;

– phase 2: learning and testing, where a classifier is learned from the training data with the best feature subset and is tested on the test data.

Given a predefined classifier, a typical wrapper model (see Figure 7.2) will perform the following steps:

1) searching a subset of features;

2) evaluating the selected subset of features by the performance of the classifier;

3) repeating Step 1 and Step 2 until the desired quality is reached.

Classification algorithms used for feature selection are often the classical ones. We may cite KNN (K-nearest neighbors), maximum likelihood classifier, Naive Bayes, support vector machine (SVM) and decision trees (see Chapter 6).

7.1.3. *Embedded models*

Embedded methods are similar to wrapper methods in the sense that the search of an optimal subset is performed for a specific learning algorithm, but they are characterized by a deeper interaction between feature selection and classifier construction.

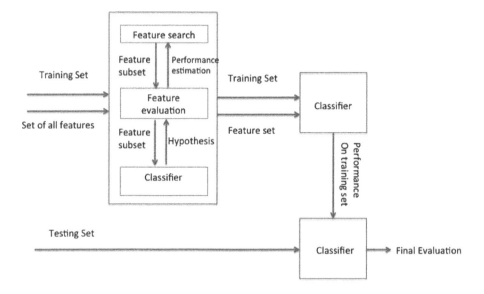

Figure 7.2. *Wrapper model for feature selection.*

7.2. Optimization model

7.2.1. *A combinatorial optimization problem*

The feature selection problem is easy to represent as a combinatorial optimization problem where the purpose is to select a subset of features for which a feature-subset evaluation criterion is optimized. Binary values of the variables x_i are used to indicate the presence ($x_i = 1$) or the absence ($x_i = 0$) of the feature i in the optimal feature set. Then, the problem is formulated as:

$$max_{x=(x_1,...,x_n)\in\{0;1\}^n} F(x)$$

for a function F that has to be determined regarding the context (filter, wrapper or embedded approach and application under study).

The optimal feature selection problem has been shown to be NP-hard [NAR 77].

In filter approaches, many different statistical feature selection measures, such as the correlation feature selection (CFS) measure, the minimal-redundancy-maximal-relevance (mRMR) measure, the discriminant function or the Mahalanobis distance, have been used to assign to each feature a score.

In wrapper approaches, classification algorithms may be used to assign to a selection of features a score that represents the ability of the selection to lead to a correct classification.

7.2.2. *Representation*

In [FRE 08], some classical representations for feature selection with metaheuristics are discussed.

The most standard representation found in the literature consists of a string of N bits, where N is the number of original attributes and each bit can take the value 1 or 0, indicating whether or not the attribute is selected. This individual representation is simple and operators can be easily applied as binary representation is very classical for metaheuristics. However, the main disadvantage of this representation is that it could have a scalability problem when the number of features increases and thus is not well-adapted to Big Data.

An alternative representation has been proposed by [CHE 96]. It consists of a fixed length representation of size M (where M is a user-specified parameter), which contains either the index of an attribute or a flag denoting no attribute. An attribute is considered selected if and only if it occurs at least one time in the solution. For instance, the solution "10310", where $M = 5$, represents a candidate solution where only the first and the third attributes are selected. The fact that the first attribute occurs twice in the individual is irrelevant for the purpose of decoding the individual into a selected attribute subset. One advantage of this representation is that it scales up better with respect to a large number of original features, since the value of M can be much smaller than the number of original features. One disadvantage is that it introduces a new parameter M.

To overcome this disadvantage, some authors propose to use a variable length representation where the solution contains only the list of selected attributes [GAR 09a].

These three different representations are illustrated in Figure 7.3.

7.2.3. *Operators*

The binary representation has often been used because it implies simplicity in operator implementation. Some authors introduce a bias in the mutation: as in feature selection the objective is to reduce the number of selected features, the mutation operator may favor the reduction by increasing the chance of mutating a gene to indicate that the feature is not selected [JUL 05, JOU 01].

a)   1 0 1 0 0 0 1 0 1 0

b)   1 3 0 7 9 1

c)   1 3 7 9

Figure 7.3. *Some representations for metaheuristic in feature selection for the selection of attributes 1,3,7,9. a) binary representation; b) fixed length representation; c) variable length representation*

A specific crossover for feature selection is the subset size-oriented common feature crossover operator (SSOCF) that aims to keep useful informative blocks and produces offspring that have the same distribution as the parents [EMM 00]. The shared features are kept by offspring and the non-shared features are inherited by the offspring corresponding to the ith parent with the probability $(n_i - n_c/n_u)$, where n_i is the number of selected features of the ith parent, n_c is the number of commonly selected features across both parents and n_u is the number of non-shared selected features.

7.2.4. *Quality measures*

Quality measures are specific to each kind of approach for feature selection: filter or wrapper/embedded.

7.2.4.1. *Filter approaches*

In filter approaches, the measure should be fast to compute. Popular filter metrics for classification problems are correlation and mutual information that computes the quality of a candidate feature (or set of features). Some other common measures are χ^2-statistic, F-statistic, Fisher criterion, entropy-based measure, the pointwise mutual information, Relief and ReliefF, Pearson product-moment correlation coefficient, inter/intra-class distance or the scores of significance tests for each class/feature combination.

7.2.4.2. *Wrapper approaches*

For supervised learning, the primary goal of classification is to maximize predictive accuracy; therefore, in wrapper approaches, predictive accuracy is generally accepted and widely used as the primary measure by researchers and practitioners.

We can distinguish different aims in the fitness functions. Some of them try to reduce the cardinality of the feature set by counting the number of features directly or by using a ratio of the cardinality of the subset over the cardinality of the global set of features. When the classifier used classification rules, some authors try to reduce the number of rule or the size of the classification tree to have a more concise model [PAP 04].

For wrapper models, the majority of fitness functions try to minimize the error rate of the used classifier. The error rate can globally be computed [LIU 01, LIU 02, ZHA 05, BOR 05], computed on the testing set [SHI 04] or computed by using cross-validation accuracy [JUL 05, HUE 06]. For binary classification, some specific measures like sensibility and specificity [EMM 02, GAR 09a] can be used. Some authors associate sensibility and specificity by computing the area under the ROC curve (AUC) that is of particular interest on medical application and imbalance classification [YAN 13].

For specific applications, authors also use specific domain fitness functions.

The feature selection problem is inherently a multiple objective problem where the objective is to have the minimum number of features that give the most accurate model of classification. More and more works propose aggregations of criteria but also pure multi-objective modelizations.

Main objective	Criteria	References
Size of the subset	Feature cardinality	[LIU 01, LIU 02, JUL 05, BAL 95, YAN 13]
Size of the model	Size of the tree	[PAP 04]
Quality of the classification model	Global error rate	[LIU 01, LIU 02, ZHA 05, BOR 05]
	Prediction	[SHI 04]
	Cross-validation accuracy	[JUL 05, HUE 06]
	Accuracy	[BAL 95]
	Sensibility	[EMM 02, GAR 09a]
	Specificity	[EMM 02, GAR 09a]
	AUC	[YAN 13]
Application-specific criteria	Gamma test value	[CHU 98]

Table 7.1. *Overview of fitness function for feature selection in classification*

7.2.4.3. *Aggregation approaches*

Two main objectives are often associated: minimizing the error rate and minimizing the number of selected features. To aggregate the two objectives, parameters to control the trade-off between preferences for each objective are used.

7.2.4.4. *Multi-objective approaches*

As reported by Kim *et al.*, traditional approaches to feature selection with a single criterion have shown some limitations [KIM 02] and more and more works use the strength of evolutionary computation for multi-objective optimization of feature selection for classification. As for aggregation approaches, the objectives are often the maximization of the quality of the classifier for wrapper methods and the minimization of the number of selected features. In [EMM 02], the authors proposed a multi-objective modelization and resolution that maximize the cross-validation accuracy on the training set and the classification accuracy on the testing set but minimize the cardinality of the feature subset. To solve the problem, the authors use NSGA-II. NSGA-II is also used in [HAM 07] where two objectives are optimized: reducing the number of selected features and classification error using the 1-NN classifier.

In [EMM 00], ELSA (evolutionary local selection algorithm), inspired from artificial life models of adaptive agents, is designed to cope with this multi-objective problem. Another multi-objective approach may be found in García-Nieto *et al.* where a multi-objective genetic algorithm is used for cancer diagnosis from gene selection in microarray datasets [GAR 09a]. In [XUE 13], PSO are adapted to multi-objective feature selection. DE has also been used for multi-objective feature selection [GAR 09b].

7.2.5. *Validation*

Performance assessments are realized by often using the same quality measure as those defined in the possible fitness function. Usually, authors realize cross-validation when the number of instances is small in comparison to the number of attributes.

As feature selection is inherently multi-objective, authors compare their results in both number of selected attributes and obtained accuracy.

7.3. Overview of methods

Various metaheuristics have been used to deal with feature selection and a survey can be found in [DIA 15].

GA are the most investigated metaheuristics [SIE 89, SKL 96, YAN 08, BAL 95, SHA 04, ALB 07a], but other paradigms are also used. Both single solution-based and population-based metaheuristics have been proposed.

In single solution-based metaheuristics, Hill climbing [CAR 94], simulated annealing (SA) [EKB 11, MEI 06, DEB 97], random search (RS) [STR 04], scatter search (SS) [LOP 06], harmony search (HS) [DIA 12] and Tabu Search (TS) [HED 08, TAH 04a, ZHA 02, TAH 04b, WAN 09, PAC 09] have been used. Hill climbing and simulated annealing suffer from two major disadvantages. First, they often converge towards local optima and, second, they can be very sensitive to the initial solution.

In population-based metaheuristics, all the paradigms have been used from classical genetic programming (GP) [MUN 06, GRA 98], memetic algorithm

(MA) [ZHU 07, XIO 10], ant colony optimization (ACO) [KAN 08, CHE 10, JEN 06, KAN 07, GOO 09, SIV 07] to bat algorithm (BA) [NAK 12, ROD 14] and particle swarm optimization (PSO) [ALB 07a, TU 07, CHU 08, LIU 11].

Hybrid approaches such as hybrids between GA-PSO [ATY 12] and ACO-GA [NEM 09] have also been proposed. Moreover, there also exist several approaches that have embedded local search procedures [KAB 12, OH 04].

Table 7.2, extracted from J. Hamon's PhD thesis [HAM 13], presents metaheuristics-based feature selection algorithms with a focus on a specific area: genomic studies. The interest of feature selection in genomics is that a large number of metaheuristics have been used to deal with a huge number of available data. Feature selection in genomic data can be considered as a first step for Big Data as the number of features is very large.

7.4. Conclusion

There are numerous approaches proposed in this chapter for feature selection in classification using metaheuristics. A lot of authors note that the performance of the feature selection in wrapper algorithms relies on the chosen classification algorithm, but can be very expensive especially when the volume of data is very large.

The objective functions used and their number also play an important role in the quality of the results obtained.

To deal with Big Data, wrapper methods should be enhanced as they are very expensive and particular attention should be paid to how to speed up the search by incorporating new mechanisms in the metaheuristics.

A classical way is parallelism and for Big Data, more and more attention is given to feature selection via Hadoop [FER 13, FER 15].

Application	Algorithm	Approach	Classifier	Evaluation Function	Reference
SNPs	Feature selection	Feature Similarity	Filter	r^2	[PHU 05]
SNPs	Genetic algorithm	Wrapper	Decision tree	Classification accuracy (10-fold)	[SHA 04]
SNPs	Hill climbing	Filter + Wrapper	Naive Bayesian	Predicted residual sum of squares	[LON 07]
SNPs	Simulated annealing		Naive Bayesian	Classification accuracy (5-fold)	[UST 11]
Segments parole	Ant colony	Wrapper	Artificial neural network	MSE	[ALA 05]
Marketing	Simulated annealing	Wrapper	Regression	AIC, r^2	[MEI 06]
Economy	Simulated annealing, Genetic algorithm	Wrapper	Regression	BIC	[KAP 05]
Spectral mass	Genetic algorithm	Wrapper	Multiple regression linear, Partial least square	Root-mean-square error of prediction	[BRO 97]
Microarray	Tabu Search + PSO	Wrapper	Support vector machine, K-nearest neighbor	Euclidian distance	[CHU 09]
Microarray	PSO + Genetic algorithm	Wrapper	Support vector machine	Classification accuracy (10-fold)	[ALB 07a]
Microarray	Genetic algorithm + Iterated Local Search	Embedded	Support vector machine	Classification accuracy (10-fold)	[DUV 09]
Microarray	Iterated Local Search	Wrapper	Regression	Posterior probability	[HAN 07c]
Microarray	Genetic algorithm	Wrapper	K-nearest neighbor	Classification accuracy (Leave-one-out cross-validation)	[JIR 05]
Microarray	Hybrid genetic algorithm	Hybrid	K-nearest neighbor	Classification accuracy (Leave-one-out cross-validation)	[OH 04]
Microarray	Genetic algorithm	Wrapper	Support vector machine	Sensibility Specificity	[XUA 11]
Microarray	Genetic algorithm	Wrapper	All paired. Support vector machine	Classification accuracy (Leave-one-out cross-validation)	[PEN 03]
Microarray	Genetic algorithm	Embedded	Support vector machine	Classification accuracy (10-fold)	[HER 07]
Microarray	Genetic algorithm	Hybrid	Support vector machine	Classification accuracy (Leave-one-out cross-validation)	[HUE 06]
Microarray	Genetic algorithm		Support vector machine	Classification accuracy (10-fold)	[MUN 06]
Microarray	Genetic algorithm	Wrapper	Support vector machine	EH-DIALL, CLUMP	[JOU 04]

Table 7.2. Overview of evolutionary feature selection applications from [HAM 13]

8

Frameworks

The objective of this chapter is to briefly present the tools available for a computer scientist or data scientist to implement their own data mining algorithms based on metaheuristics by using metaheuristics frameworks. Some classical data mining tools are also described to compare their results with other approaches. In the first section, generalities on frameworks to design metaheuristics and some well-known algorithms are presented. In section 8.2, a brief overview on open-source data mining frameworks is given. In the last section, some frameworks that already use metaheuristics to solve data mining tasks are presented.

8.1. Frameworks for designing metaheuristics

Frameworks are useful tools that can speed up the development of optimization-based problem solving projects, reducing their development time and costs. They may also be applied by non-expert users as well to extend the user base and the applications scope for metaheuristics techniques. Many frameworks are available, which overlap and provide similar capabilities. There are many surveys that propose a comparison of frameworks for developing metaheuristics [WOO 02, WIL 04, GAG 06]. Authors often provide a new framework or a new version of their framework. Some of them provide a complete survey and comparison [PAR 12]. There are numerous frameworks: Comet, EvA2, evolvica, Evolutionary::Algorithm, GAPlayground, jaga, JCLEC, JGAP, jMetal, n-genes, Open Beagle, Opt4j, ParadisEO/EO, Pisa, Watchmaker, FOM, Hypercube, HotFrame, Templar, EasyLocal, iOpt, OptQuest, JDEAL, Optimization Algorithm Toolkit,

HeuristicLab, MAFRA, Localizer, GALIB, DREAM, Discropt, MALLBA, MAGMA and UOF. Some frameworks that can appear in some surveys seem to be no longer used: jaga, hotframe, templar, MAFRA, DREAM, Discropt and UOF.

In this chapter, we briefly present some of the most widely used frameworks by the community and focus on a small part of the frameworks, and a comparison extracted from [PAR 12] is presented in Table 8.1.

Name	Prog. Lang.	Platforms	License	Web
EasyLocal++[DIG 03]	C++	Unix	GPL	https://bitbucket.org/satt/easylocal-3
ECJ [LUK 09]	Java	All	Open Source[1]	http://cs.gmu.edu/eclab/projects/ecj/
ParadisEO [CAH 04b]	C++	All [2]	CECILL	http://paradiseo.gforge.inria.fr
HeuristicLab [WAG 09]	C#	Windows	GPL	http://dev.heuristiclab.com
JCLEC [VEN 08]	Java	All	LGPL	http://JCLEC.sourceforge.net
jMetal [DUR 11]	Java	All	Open Source	http://jmetal.github.io/jMetal/
MALLBA [ALB 07b]	C++	Unix	Open source	http://neo.lcc.uma.es/mallba/ easy-mallba/index.html

Table 8.1. *Some available frameworks*

8.1.1. *Easylocal++*

EasyLocal++ is a framework developed by the University of Udine, Italy, for modeling and solving combinatorial optimization problems through local search metaheuristics [DIG 03]. The latter is a very recent release. The framework is entirely written in C++ and makes broad use of template metaprogramming to achieve both separation of concerns and performance. The architecture of Easylocal++ provides a principled modularization for the solution of combinatorial problems by local searches and helps the user by deriving a neat conceptual scheme of the application. It also supports the design of combinations of basic techniques and/or neighborhood structures.

8.1.2. *HeuristicLab*

HeuristicLab is a framework for heuristic and evolutionary algorithms that has been developed by members of the heuristic and evolutionary algorithms laboratory (HEAL) since 2002 and available on http://dev.heuristiclab.com/. In HeuristicLab, one particular aspect is that algorithms are represented as operator graphs and changing or rearranging operators can be done by drag-and-drop without actually writing code. HeuristicLab includes the following algorithms: genetic algorithm, genetic programming, offspring selection, local search, simulated annealing, Tabu Search, particle swarm optimization and NSGA-II.

8.1.3. *jMetal*

jMetal stands for metaheuristic algorithms in Java, and it is an object-oriented Java-based framework for multi-objective optimization with metaheuristics [DUR 11, NEB 15]. jMetal includes a number of classic and modern state-of-the-art optimizers, a wide set of benchmark problems and a set of well-known quality indicators to assess the performance of the algorithms. The framework also provides support to carry out full experimental studies, which can be configured and executed by using jMetal's graphical interface. Other features include the automatic generation of statistical information of the results obtained and taking advantage of the current availability of multi-core processors to speed-up the running time of the experiments.

8.1.4. *Mallba*

The Mallba project developed by the NEO team of Malaga Spain is a library of skeletons for combinatorial optimization (including exact, heuristic and hybrid methods) that can deal with parallelism in a user-friendly and, at the same time, efficient manner [ALB 07b] . Its three target environments are sequential computers, LANs of workstations and WANs. The main features of Mallba are:

– integration of all the skeletons under the same design principles;

– facility to switch from sequential to parallel optimization engines. By providing sequential implementations, users obtain parallel implementations;

– cooperation between engines makes possible to provide more powerful hybrid engines;

– ready to use on commodity machines;

– flexible and extensible software architecture. New skeletons can easily be added, alternative communication layers can be used, etc.

This framework seems to be old and less and less used.

8.1.5. *ParadisEO*

ParadisEO is a white-box object-oriented framework dedicated to the reusable design of metaheuristics, hybrid metaheuristics and parallel and distributed metaheuristics [CAH 04b]. ParadisEO provides a broad range of features including evolutionary algorithms, local searches, particle swarm optimization, the most common parallel and distributed models, hybridization mechanisms, etc. ParadisEO is based on a clear conceptual separation of the solution methods from the problems they are intended to solve. This separation confers to the user a maximum code and design reuse. ParadisEO is a compound of several boxes: Paradiseo-EO, Paradiseo-MOEO, Paradiseo-MO and Paradiseo-PEO.

Paradiseo-EO deals with population-based metaheuristics, it is a template-based, ANSI-C++ compliant evolutionary computation library (evolutionary algorithms, particle swarm optimization, etc.).

Paradiseo-MOEO provides a broad range of tools for the design of multi-objective optimization metaheuristics: fitness assignment schemes (achievement functions, ranking, indicator-based, etc.), diversity preservation mechanisms (sharing and crowding), elitism, performance metrics (contribution, entropy, etc.), statistical tools and some easy-to-use state-of-the-art multi-objective evolutionary algorithms (NSGA, NSGA-II, IBEA, etc.) [LIE 11].

Paradiseo-MO deals with single-solution based metaheuristics and provides tools for the development of single solution-based metaheuristics: hill climbing, Tabu Search, iterative local search (ILS), simulated annealing, incremental evaluation, partial neighborhood, etc. [HUM 13].

Paradiseo-PEO provides tools for the design of parallel and distributed metaheuristics: parallel evaluation, parallel evaluation function, island model, cellular model, etc. Paradiseo-PEO also introduces tools for the design of distributed, hybrid and cooperative models [CAH 04a].

8.1.6. *ECJ*

ECJ is a generic toolkit in Java aimed at all forms of evolutionary computation. In addition to GP, it supports GA, evolutionary strategies, PSO and differential evolution, available on http://cs.gmu.edu/ eclab/projects/ecj//. However, GP is one of its strongest suits and correspondingly ECJ supports many useful GP features. ECJ supports multi-thread evaluation and breeding, a master-slave architecture, island models and even experimental support for GPGPU through a third-party extension. A larger review is available in [WHI 12].

8.1.7. *OpenBeagle*

OpenBeagle [GAG 06] is a C++ Evolutionary Computation framework available at http://chgagne.github.io/beagle/. It provides a high-level software environment. Its architecture follows strong principles of object-oriented programming, where abstractions are represented by loosely coupled objects and it is common and easy to reuse code.

OpenBeagle includes bit string representation with decoder functions (binary and Gray-coded), integer-valued vector representation indices permutation vector representation, real-valued vector GA representation, anisotropic self-adaptive evolution strategy (SA-ES), covariance matrix adaptation ES (CMA-ES), multi-objective optimization (including NSGA-II), complete implementation of tree-based GP automatically defined functions (ADF) for GP, constrained GP tree operators with support for strongly typed GP, co-evolution support based on multi-threading.

8.1.8. *JCLEC*

JCLEC is a software system for evolutionary computation (EC) research, developed in the Java programming language http://jclec.sourceforge.net/. It provides a high-level software framework to perform any kind of evolutionary algorithm (EA), providing support for genetic algorithms (binary, integer and real encoding), genetic programming (Koza's style, strongly typed and grammar based) and evolutionary programming. *KEEL* is presented in section 8.3.3.

8.2. Framework for data mining

We briefly present some popular frameworks without metaheuristics that can be used to compare results obtained by metaheuristics-based data mining algorithms. In the following, we only focus on freely available frameworks. Propriety vendor data mining software include IBM SPSS modeler, SAS Enterprise Miner, Oracle Data Mining, IBM DB2 Intelligent Miner, Statistica Data miner, etc.

Area	ECJ	ParadisEO	EasyLocal	HeuristicLab	MALLBA	Avg (/12)
Supported metaheuristics	0.207	0.381	0.264	0.324	0.245	0.282
Problem adaptation/encoding	0.254	0.413	0.150	0.484	0.102	0.249
Advanced metaheuristic characteristics	0.400	0.500	0.100	0.300	0.367	0.226
Optimization process support	0.368	0.192	0.165	0.458	0.131	0.356
Design, implementation and licensing	0.905	0.797	0.717	0.708	0.417	0.786
Documentation, samples and popularity	0.789	0.348	0.094	0.340	0.177	0.304
Parallelism	Yes	Yes			Yes	
Average per framework	0.487	0.439	0.248	0.436	0.240	0.367

Table 8.2. *A comparison of frameworks extracted from [PAR 12]. The average has been computed over 12 frameworks*

Name	Prog. Lang.	Platforms	Metaheuristics?	License	Web
Orange	Python/C++	All	No	Open Source (GPLv3)	http://orange.biolab.si/
Rattle GUI	R	All	No	Free (GPLv2+)	http://rattle.togaware.com/
Rapid Miner	Java	All	Yes	Open source (GPLv3)	https://rapidminer.com/
WEKA	Java	All	Yes	Open source (GPLv3)	http://www.cs.waikato.ac.nz/ml/weka/index.html
KEEL	Java	All	Yes	Open source (GPLv3)	http://sci2s.ugr.es/keel/
Mo-Mine	C++	All	Yes	Open source	http://mo-mine.gforge.inria.fr/

Table 8.3. *A comparison of frameworks for data mining*

8.2.1. *Orange*

Orange is an open source data visualization and analysis tool [DEM 13]. Orange is developed by the Bioinformatics Lab at the University of Ljubljana, Slovenia, in collaboration with the open-source community. Data mining can be done through a very friendly visual interface or directly by python scripting. All the basic data mining tasks are available: classification, regression, feature selection, rule mining and clustering. In Figure 8.2, an example of the visualization of the results with Orange is depicted. There are no metaheuristics available in the software. The software can be downloaded from http://orange.biolab.si/.

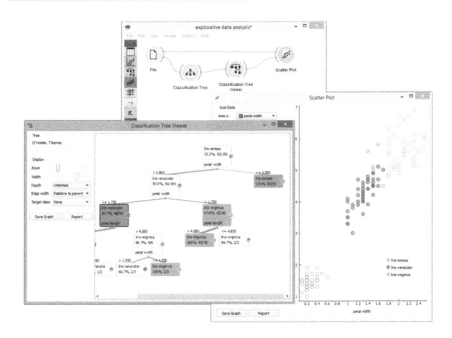

Figure 8.1. *Clustering and tree exploration with Orange*

8.2.2. *R and Rattle GUI*

Rattle GUI is a free and open source software from Togaware, providing a graphical user interface (GUI) for data mining using R statistical programming language [WIL 11]. Rattle provides considerable data mining functionality by exposing the power of the R statistical software through a simple GUI (see Figure 8.2). All data mining tools can be realized, thanks to Rattle: clustering, association rule mining and decision trees classification. There is no metaheuristics available in the software. The software can be downloaded from http://rattle.togaware.com/

8.3. Framework for data mining with metaheuristics

Recently, several commercial data mining tools have been developed based on soft computing methodologies and, in particular, metaheuristics like Nuggets [MIT 02] http://www.data-mine.com/solutions/nuggets and GATrees http://www.gatree.com/ [PAP 00, KAL 10] using genetic algorithms. Only open source solutions are presented below.

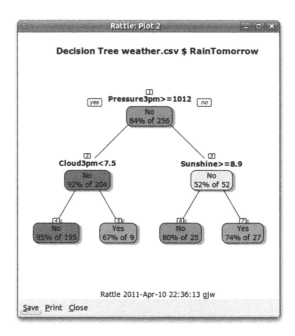

Figure 8.2. *Tree exploration with Rattle GUI*

8.3.1. *RapidMiner*

RapidMiner provides an integrated environment for machine learning, data mining and text mining. RapidMiner supports all steps of the data mining process and provides a GUI to design and execute analytical workflow. For example, in RapidMiner, genetic algorithms are used to realize feature selection, support vector machine (SVM) uses PSO for optimization of the parameters. An example of the GUI for tree exploration is shown in Figure 8.3. The software can be downloaded from https://rapidminer.com/.

8.3.2. *WEKA*

WEKA is a collection of machine learning algorithms for data mining written in Java and developed at the University of Waikato in New Zealand [HAL 09]. The algorithms can be applied directly on a dataset through a GUI or included in a Java code. An example of the GUI of WEKA is shown in Figure 8.4. WEKA contains tools for data preprocessing, classification, regression, clustering, association rules and visualization. WEKA was the first widely used data mining software that includes metaheuristics in the proposed machine learning algorithms. Metaheuristics are mainly used in WEKA to realize feature selection. For example, attribute selection can be realized, thanks to a Tabu Search and the implementation in WEKA has been based on [HED 08]. There is also a genetic algorithm-based feature selection. Different contributors have developed metaheuristics-based component that can be added to WEKA.

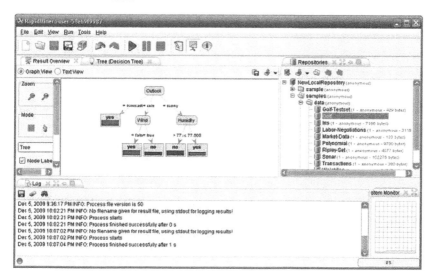

Figure 8.3. *Tree exploration with RapidMiner*

The software can be downloaded from http://www.cs.waikato.ac.nz/ml/weka/index.html.

8.3.3. *KEEL*

Knowledge extraction based on evolutionary learning (KEEL) is an open-source (GPLv3) Java software tool that can be used for a large number of different knowledge data discovery tasks [ALC 09a, ALC 11] and available on http://sci2s.ugr.es/keel/. This software tool is available to assess evolutionary algorithms for data mining problems of various kinds including regression, classification, unsupervised learning, etc. It includes evolutionary learning algorithms based on different approaches: Pittsburgh, Michigan, as well as the integration of evolutionary learning techniques with different preprocessing techniques, allowing us to perform a complete analysis of any learning model in comparison to existing software tools. KEEL is very powerful with a user-friendly GUI. Some algorithms have been developed by using a Java class library for evolutionary computation (JCLEC) 8.1.8.

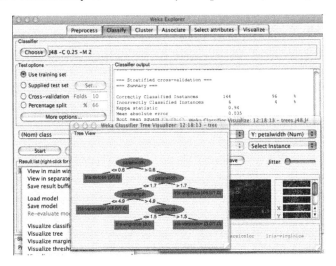

Figure 8.4. *Decision tree with WEKA*

It contains a knowledge extraction algorithms library, remarking the incorporation of multiple evolutionary learning algorithms, together with classical learning approaches. The main features are:

– various evolutionary rule learning models;

– fuzzy rule learning models with a good trade-off between accuracy and interpretability;

– evolution and pruning in neural networks, product unit neural networks and radial base models;

– genetic programming: evolutionary algorithms that use tree representations for extracting knowledge;

– algorithms for extracting descriptive rules based on pattern subgroup discovery have been integrated;

– data reduction (training set selection, feature selection and discretization). EAs for data reduction have been included.

8.3.4. *MO-Mine*

MO-Mine is a recent library that allows us to process tests and evaluations of multi-objective optimization algorithms for data mining developed by Inria/University of Lille France, available on http://mo-mine.gforge.inria.fr/. MO-Mine provides data preprocessing methods (attribute selection), data mining (clustering, classification and association rules) algorithms based on multi-objective metaheuristics (evolutionary algorithm), validation methods and tools to compare algorithms. MO-Mine proposes to users to compare their own methods with different approaches, following protocols clearly identified and shared [FIS 15].

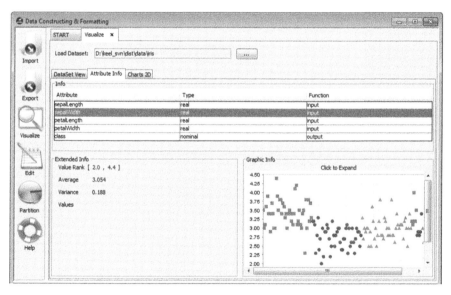

Figure 8.5. *LIONoso*

8.4. Conclusion

Many frameworks exist to develop metaheuristics. However, some are more mature than others and their possibilities are quite different in terms of metaheuristics provided, parallel possible implementations, documentation, etc.

The same remarks can be made to data mining frameworks, but they are often easier to handle than metaheuristics frameworks. We have observed that more and more data mining frameworks offer the possibility of using metaheuristics but often in their simplest version. Many data mining frameworks are open source with a large community of users and their implementation uses classical programming languages (Java, C++) that should lead to research in the field of data mining with metaheuristics to provide implementation of their methods in the mentioned frameworks.

Conclusion

The question:

Big Data: a buzzword or a real challenge?

This book has shown that challenges exist within the context of Big Data. Although difficult, dealing with various sources of data offers exciting opportunities for increasing knowledge and improving decisions in many application fields. Nowadays, scientists from different domains – medicine, genomics, physics, biology, chemistry, electrical or mechanical engineering, etc. – and also decision makers from the industry have more and more data to exploit in order to be competitive.

While focusing on the data analytics phase (which is a single phase among several others), there are still numerous challenges to deal with Big Data. Metaheuristics have been widely used to address one or the other data mining tasks. They have shown a good ability to tackle some of the challenges. Their flexibility makes them easily adaptable to different types of data, different contexts and different questions.

Thus, Big Data offers a great experimentation field for metaheuristics design, as it offers many different situations. And this is only the beginning. The Internet of Things will still generate more and more data, more and more rapidly, at different places. This will create many opportunities to design new efficient metaheuristics. Even more flexibility and self-adaptation of methods will be the key success factors.

Bibliography

[AGR 93] AGRAWAL R., IMIELINSKI T., SWAMI A.N., "Mining association rules between sets of items in large databases", *Proceedings of the 1993 ACM SIGMOD International Conference on Management of Data*, ACM Press, pp. 207–216, 1993.

[AGR 94] AGRAWAL R., SRIKANT R., "Fast algorithms for mining association rules in large databases", *VLDB '94: Proceedings of the 20th International Conference on Very Large Databases*, Morgan Kaufmann Publishers Inc., pp. 487–499, 1994.

[ALA 05] AL-ANI A., "Ant colony optimization for feature subset selection", *WEC, World Academy of Science, Engineering and* Technology, pp. 35–38, 2005.

[ALA 08] ALATAS B., AKIN E., KARCI A., "MODENAR: multi-objective differential evolution algorithm for mining numeric association rules", *Applied Soft Computing*, Elsevier, vol. 8, no. 1, pp. 646–656, 2008.

[ALA 12] ALATAS B., "A novel chemistry-based metaheuristic optimization method for mining of classification rules", *Expert Systems with Applications*, Elsevier, vol. 39, no. 12, pp. 11080–11088, 2012.

[ALA 14] ALAM S., DOBBIE G., KOH Y. *et al.*, "Research on particle swarm optimization based clustering: a systematic review of literature and techniques", *Swarm and Evolutionary Computation*, vol. 17, pp. 1–13, 2014.

[ALB 05] ALBA E., TALBI E.-G., LUQUE G. *et al.*, "*Parallel metaheuristics: a new class of algorithms*", Wiley Series on Parallel and Distributed Computing, Wiley, Chapter 4, Metaheuristics and parallelism, pp. 79–104, 2005.

[ALB 07a] ALBA E., GARCÍA-NIETO J., JOURDAN L. *et al.*, "Gene selection in cancer classification using PSO/SVM and GA/SVM hybrid algorithms", *IEEE Congress on Evolutionary Computation*, IEEE, pp. 284–290, 2007.

[ALB 07b] ALBA E., LUQUE G., GARCÍA-NIETO J. *et al.*, "MALLBA: a software library to design efficient optimization algorithms", *Int. J. Innov. Comput. Appl.*, Inderscience Publishers, vol. 1, no. 1, pp. 74–85, April 2007.

[ALB 13] ALBA E., LUQUE G., NESMACHNOW S., "Parallel metaheuristics: recent advances and new trends", *International Transactions in Operational Research*, vol. 20, no. 1, pp. 1–48, 2013.

[ALC 09a] ALCALÁ-FDEZ J., SÁNCHEZ L., GARCÍA S. *et al.*, "KEEL: a software tool to assess evolutionary algorithms for data mining problems", *Soft Computing*, Springer-Verlag, vol. 13, no. 3, pp. 307–318, 2009.

[ALC 09b] ALCALÁ-FDEZ J., ALCALÁ R., GACTO M.J. *et al.*, "Learning the membership function contexts for mining fuzzy association rules by using genetic algorithms", *Fuzzy Sets and Systems*, Elsevier, vol. 160, no. 7, pp. 905–921, 2009.

[ALC 11] ALCALÁ-FDEZ J., FERNÁNDEZ A., LUENGO J. *et al.*, "KEEL Data mining software tool: data set repository, integration of algorithms and experimental analysis framework", *Multiple-valued Logic and Soft Computing*, vol. 17, nos. 2–3, pp. 255–287, 2011.

[ALM 89] ALMASI G.S., GOTTLIEB A., *Highly parallel computing*, Benjamin-Cummings Publishing Co., Inc., Redwood City, CA, USA, 1989.

[ÁLV 12] ÁLVAREZ V.P., VÁZQUEZ J.M., "An evolutionary algorithm to discover quantitative association rules from huge databases without the need for an *a priori* discretization", *Expert systems with applications*, Elsevier, vol. 39, no. 1, pp. 585–593, 2012.

[ANA 09] ANAND R., VAID A., SINGH P.K., "Association rule mining using multi-objective evolutionary algorithms: strengths and challenges", *World Congress on Nature and Biologically Inspired Computing (NaBIC)*, IEEE, pp. 385–390, 2009.

[ANT 12] ANTONELLI M., DUCANGE P., MARCELLONI F., "Multi-objective evolutionary rule and condition selection for designing fuzzy rule-based classifiers", *IEEE International Conference onFuzzy systems (FUZZ-IEEE)*, IEEE, pp. 1–7, 2012.

[ATY 12] ATYABI A., LUERSSEN M., FITZGIBBON S. *et al.*, "Evolutionary feature selection and electrode reduction for EEG classification", *IEEE Congress on Evolutionary Computation (CEC)* IEEE, pp. 1–8, 2012.

[BAC 07] BACARDIT J., BUTZ M.V., "Data mining in learning classifier systems: comparing XCS with GAssist", *Learning classifier Systems*, Springer, vol. 4399, pp. 282–290, 2007.

[BAL 95] BALA J., HUANG J., VAFAIE H. *et al.*, "Hybrid learning using genetic algorithms and decision trees for pattern classification", *IJCAI (1)*, pp. 719–724, 1995.

[BAN 01] BANDYOPADHYAY S., MAULIK U., "Non-parametric genetic clustering: comparison of validity indices", *IEEE Transactions on Systems, Man and Cybernetics Part C: Applications and Reviews*, vol. 31, no. 1, pp. 120–125, 2001.

[BAN 07] BANDYOPADHYAY S., MUKHOPADHYAY A., MAULIK U., "An improved algorithm for clustering gene expression data", *Bioinformatics*, vol. 23, no. 21, pp. 2859–2865, 2007.

[BAR 12] BARROS R.C., BASGALUPP M.P., DE CARVALHO A.C. *et al.*, "A hyper-heuristic evolutionary algorithm for automatically designing decision tree algorithms", *Proceedings of the 14th Annual Conference on Genetic and Evolutionary Computation*, ACM, pp. 1237–1244, 2012.

[BAS 06] BASSEUR M., ZTZLER E., "Handling uncertainty in indicator-based multiobjective optimization", *International Journal of Computational Intelligence Research*, vol. 2, no. 3, pp. 255–272, 2006.

[BAS 15] BASGALUPP M.P., BARROS R.C., PODGORELEC V., "Evolving decision tree induction algorithms with a multi-objective hyper-heuristic", *Proceedings of the 30th Annual ACM Symposium on Applied Computing*, ACM, pp. 110–117, 2015.

[BEN 13] BEN SAID Z., GUILLET F., RICHARD P. *et al.*, "Visualisation of association rules based on a molecular representation", *17th International Conference Information visualisation (IV)*, pp. 577–581, July 2013.

[BER 87] BERGMANN B., HOMMEL G., "Improvements of general multiple test procedures for redundant systems of hypotheses", *Proc. Symp. on Multiple Hypotheses Testing*, Springer, Berlin, pp. 100–115, 1987.

[BEU 07] BEUME N., NAUJOKS B., EMMERICH M., "SMS-EMOA: multi-objective selection based on dominated hypervolume", *European Journal of Operational Research*, Elsevier, vol. 181, no. 3, pp. 1653–1669, 2007.

[BEY 12] BEYER M.A., LANEY D., "The importance of 'Big Data': a definition", *Stamford, CT: gartner*, pp. 2014–2018, 2012.

[BEY 13] BEYER H.-G., *The theory of evolution strategies*, Springer Science & Business Media, Berlin, 2013.

[BEZ 94] BEZDEK J.C., BOGGAVARAPU S., HALL L.O. *et al.*, "Genetic algorithm guided clustering", *International Conference on Evolutionary Computation*, pp. 34–39, 1994.

[BLU 03] BLUM C., ROLI A., "Metaheuristics in combinatorial optimization: overview and conceptual comparison", *ACM Computing Surveys (CSUR)*, vol. 35, no. 3, pp. 268–308, ACM, 2003.

[BON 99] BONABEAU E., DORIGO M., THERAULAZ G., *Swarm intelligence: from natural to artificial systems*, No. 1, Oxford University Press, Oxford, 1999.

[BON 11] BONG C.-W., RAJESWARI M., "Multi-objective nature-inspired clustering and classification techniques for image segmentation", *Applied Soft Computing Journal*, vol. 11, no. 4, pp. 3271–3282, 2011.

[BOR 03] BORGELT C., "Efficient implementations of *A* priori and *Eclat*", *Proc. 1st IEEE ICDM Workshop on Frequent Item Set Mining Implementations (FIMI 2003)*, p. 90, 2003.

[BOR 05] BORGES H.B., NIEVOLA J.C., "Attribute selection methods comparison for classification of diffuse large B-cell lymphoma", *Proceedings: Fourth International Conference on Machine Learning and Applications*, IEEE, pp. 6, 2005.

[BOR 10] BORYCZKA U., KOZAK J., "Ant colony decision trees-a new method for constructing decision trees based on ant colony optimization", *Technologies and Applications Computational Collective Intelligence*, Springer, pp. 373–382, 2010.

[BOR 15] BORYCZKA U., KOZAK J., "Enhancing the effectiveness of ant colony decision tree algorithms by co-learning", *Applied Soft Computing*, Elsevier, vol. 30, pp. 166–178, 2015.

[BOU 13] BOUSSAÏD I., LEPAGNOT J., SIARRY P., "A survey on optimization metaheuristics", *Information Sciences*, vol. 237, pp. 82–117, Elsevier, 2013.

[BRE 84] BREIMAN L., FRIEDMAN J.H., OLSHEN R.A. *et al.*, *Classification and regression trees*, Wadsworth international, Belmont, CA, 1984.

[BRO 97] BROADHURST D., GOODACRE R., JONES A. *et al.*, "Genetic algorithms as a method for variable selection in multiple linear regression and partial least squares regression, with applications to pyrolysis mass spectrometry", *Analytica Chimica Acta*, pp. 71–86, 1997.

[BUR 07] BURSA M., LHOTSKA L., MACAS M., "Hybridized swarm metaheuristics for evolutionary random forest generation", *7th International Conference on Hybrid Intelligent Systems*, pp. 150–155, September 2007.

[CAH 04a] CAHON S., MELAB N. *et al.*, "Building with ParadisEO reusable parallel and distributed evolutionary algorithms", *Parallel Computing*, vol. 30, nos 5–6, pp. 677–697, 2004.

[CAH 04b] CAHON S., MELAB N., TALBI E. *et al.*, "ParadisEO: a framework for the reusable design of parallel and distributed metaheuristics", *J. Heuristics*, vol. 10, no. 3, pp. 357–380, 2004.

[CAR 94] CARUANA R., FREITAG D., "Greedy attribute selection", *ICML*, Citeseer, pp. 28–36, 1994.

[CAR 13] CARRIZOSA E., MORALES D.R., "Supervised classification and mathematical optimization", *Computers and Operations Research*, Elsevier, vol. 40, no. 1, pp. 150–165, 2013.

[CAS 09] CASILLAS J., MARTINEZ P., BENITEZ A., "Learning consistent, complete and compact sets of fuzzy rules in conjunctive normal form for regression problems", *Soft Computing-a Fusion of Foundations, Methodologies and Applications*, Springer Berlin, Heidelberg, vol. 13, pp. 451–465, 2009.

[CHE 96] CHERKAUER K.J., SHAVLIK J.W., "Growing simpler decision trees to facilitate knowledge discovery", *KDD*, Citeseer, vol. 96, pp. 315–318, 1996.

[CHE 10] CHEN Y., MIAO D., WANG R., "A rough set approach to feature selection based on ant colony optimization", *Pattern Recognition Letters*, Elsevier, vol. 31, no. 3, pp. 226–233, 2010.

[CHE 13] CHE D., SAFRAN M., PENG Z., "From Big Data to Big Data mining: challenges, issues and opportunities", *Database Systems for Advanced Applications*, Springer, pp. 1–15, 2013.

[CHE 14] CHEN M., MAO S., LIU Y., "Big Data: a survey", *Mobile Networks and Applications*, Springer, vol. 19, no. 2, pp. 171–209, 2014.

[CHU 98] CHUZHANOVA N.A., JONES A.J., MARGETTS S., "Feature selection for genetic sequence classification", *Bioinformatics*, Oxford University Press, vol. 14, no. 2, pp. 139–143, 1998.

[CHU 08] CHUANG L.-Y., CHANG H.-W., TU C.-J. *et al.*, "Improved binary PSO for feature selection using gene expression data", *Computational Biology and Chemistry*, Elsevier, vol. 32, no. 1, pp. 29–38, 2008.

[CHU 09] CHUANG L.-Y., YANG C.-H., "Tabu search and binary particle swarm optimization for feature selection using microarray data", *Journal of computational biology*, Mary Ann Liebert Inc., New Rochelle, USA, vol. 16, no. 12, pp. 1689–1703, 2009.

[COE 07] COELLO C.C., LAMONT G.B., VAN VELDHUIZEN D.A., *Evolutionary algorithms for solving multi-objective problems*, Springer Science and Business Media, Berlin, 2007.

[COE 10a] COELLO C.C., DHAENENS C., JOURDAN L., *Advances in multi-objective nature inspired computing*, vol. 272, Springer, 2010.

[COE 10b] COELLO C.C., DHAENENS C., JOURDAN L., "Multi-objective combinatorial optimization: problematic and context", *Advances in Multi-objective Nature Inspired Computing*, pp. 1–21, Springer, 2010.

[COR 95] CORTES C., VAPNIK V., "Support-vector networks", *Machine learning*, Springer, vol. 20, no. 3, pp. 273–297, 1995.

[COR 00] CORNE D.W., KNOWLES J.D., OATES M.J., "The Pareto envelope-based selection algorithm for multi-objective optimization", *Parallel problem solving from nature PPSN VI*, Springer, pp. 839–848, 2000.

[COR 12] CORNE D., DHAENENS C., JOURDAN L., "Synergies between operations research and data mining: the emerging use of multi-objective approaches", *European Journal of Operational Research*, Elsevier, vol. 221, no. 3, pp. 469–479, 2012.

[COW 99] COWGILL M., HARVEY R., WATSON L., "Genetic algorithm approach to cluster analysis", *Computers and Mathematics with Applications*, vol. 37, no. 7, pp. 99–108, 1999.

[CUL 97] CULLER D.E., GUPTA A., SINGH J.P., *Parallel computer architecture: a hardware/software approach*, Morgan Kaufmann Publishers Inc., San Francisco, 1st edition, 1997.

[DAS 08] DAS S., ABRAHAM A., KONAR A., "Swarm intelligence algorithms in bioinformatics", *Computational Intelligence in Bioinformatics*, Springer, pp. 113–147, 2008.

[DAV 79] DAVIES D.L., BOULDIN D.W., "A cluster separation measure", *IEEE Transactions on Pattern Analysis and Machine Intelligence*, vol. PAMI-1, no. 2, pp. 224–227, April 1979.

[DEA 99] DE ARAUJO D.L.A., LOPES H.S., FREITAS A. *et al.*, "A parallel genetic algorithm for rule discovery in large databases", *IEEE International Conference on systems, man and cybernetics*, vol. 3, IEEE, pp. 940–945, 1999.

[DEB 97] DEBUSE J.C., RAYWARD-SMITH V.J., "Feature subset selection within a simulated annealing data mining algorithm", *Journal of Intelligent Information systems*, vol. 9, no. 1, pp. 57–81, 1997.

[DEB 01] DEB K., *Multi-objective optimization using evolutionary algorithms*, John Wiley & Sons, New York, vol. 16, 2001.

[DEB 02] DEB K., PRATAP A., AGARWAL S. *et al.*, "A fast and elitist multiobjective genetic algorithm: NSGA-II", *IEEE Transactions on Evolutionary Computation*, IEEE, vol. 6, no. 2, pp. 182–197, 2002.

[DEH 06] DEHURI S., JAGADEV A., GHOSH A. *et al.*, "Multi-objective genetic algorithm for association rule mining using a homogeneous dedicated cluster of workstations", *American Journal of Applied Sciences*, vol. 3, no. 11, pp. 2086–2095, 2006.

[DEL 03] DELGADO M., MARIN N., SANCHEZ D. *et al.*, "Fuzzy association rules: general model and applications", *IEEE Transactions on Fuzzy Systems*, vol. 11, no. 2, pp. 214–225, April 2003.

[DEL 09] DELISLE P., KRAJECKI M., GRAVEL M., "Multi-colony parallel ant colony optimization on smp and multi-core computers", *World Congress on Nature and Biologically Inspired Computing (NaBIC)*, pp. 318–323, 2009.

[DEM 06] DEMAR J., "Statistical comparisons of classifiers over multiple data sets", *The Journal of Machine Learning Research*, vol. 7, pp. 1–30, 2006.

[DEM 13] DEMAR J., CURK T., ERJAVEC A. *et al.*, "Orange: data mining toolbox in python", *Journal of Machine Learning Research*, vol. 14, pp. 2349–2353, 2013.

[DEM 16] DE MAURO A., GRECO M., GRIMALDI M. *et al.*, "A formal definition of Big Data based on its essential features", *Library Review*, Emerald Group Publishing Limited, vol. 65, no. 3, 2016.

[DHA 10] DHAENENS C., LEMESRE J., TALBI E.-G., "K-PPM: A new exact method to solve multi-objective combinatorial optimization problems", *European Journal of Operational Research*, Elsevier, vol. 200, no. 1, pp. 45–53, 2010.

[DIA 12] DIAO R., SHEN Q., "Feature selection with harmony search", *IEEE Transactions on Systems, Man and Cybernetics, Part B: cybernetics,* IEEE, vol. 42, no. 6, pp. 1509–1523, 2012.

[DIA 15] DIAO R., SHEN Q., "Nature inspired feature selection meta-heuristics", *Artif. Intell. Rev.*, Kluwer Academic Publishers, vol. 44, no. 3, pp. 311–340, October 2015.

[DIG 03] DI GASPERO L., SCHAERF A., "EASYLOCAL++: an object-oriented framework for flexible design of local search algorithms", *Software - Practice & Experience*, John Wiley & Sons, New York, vol. 33, no. 8, pp. 733–765, July 2003.

[DJE 12] DJENOURI Y., DRIAS H., HABBAS Z. *et al.*, "Bees swarm optimization for web association rule mining", *IEEE/WIC/ACM International Conferences on Web Intelligence and Intelligent Agent Technology (WI-IAT)*, vol. 3, pp. 142–146, December 2012.

[DOR 92] DORIGO M., Optimization, learning and natural algorithms, PhD Thesis, Politecnico di Milano, Italy, 1992.

[DOR 05] DORIGO M.,BLUM C., "Ant colony optimization theory: a survey", *Theoretical Computer Science*, Elsevier, vol. 344, no. 2, pp. 243–278, 2005.

[DUC 10] DUCANGE P., LAZZERINI B., MARCELLONI F., "Multi-objective genetic fuzzy classifiers for imbalanced and cost-sensitive datasets", *Soft Computing*, Springer, vol. 14, no. 7, pp. 713–728, 2010.

[DUE 90] DUECK G., SCHEUER T., "Threshold accepting: a general purpose optimization algorithm appearing superior to simulated annealing", *Journal of Computational Physics*, vol. 90, no. 1, pp. 161–175, Elsevier, 1990.

[DUR 11] DURILLO J.J., NEBRO A.J., "jMetal: A Java framework for multi-objective optimization", *Advances in Engineering Software*, vol. 42, no. 10, pp. 760–771, 2011.

[DUV 09] DUVAL B., HAO J.-K., HERNANDEZ HERNANDEZ J.C., "A memetic algorithm for gene selection and molecular classification of cancer", *Proceedings of the 11th Annual Conference on Genetic and evolutionary computation*, ACM, pp. 201–208, 2009.

[EBE 01] EBERHART R.C., SHI Y., "Particle swarm optimization: developments, applications and resources", *Proceedings of the 2001 Congress on Evolutionary Computation*, IEEE, vol. 1, pp. 81–86, 2001.

[EDG 81] EDGEWORTH F.Y., *Mathematical psychics: an essay on the application of mathematics to the moral sciences*, No. 10, CK Paul, 1881.

[EKB 11] EKBAL A., SAHA S., URYUPINA O. *et al.*, in Chapter "Multi-objective simulated annealing based approach for feature selection in anaphora resolution", *Anaphora processing and applications: 8th discourse anaphora and anaphor resolution colloquium, DAARC 2011, Faro, Portugal, October 6–7, 2011, Revised selected papers*, pp. 47–58, Springer, 2011.

[EMM 00] EMMANOUILIDIS C., HUNTER A., MACINTYRE J., "A multi-objective evolutionary setting for feature selection and a commonality-based crossover operator", *Proceedings of the 2000 Congress on evolutionary computation*, IEEE, vol. 1, pp. 309–316, 2000.

[EMM 02] EMMANOUILIDIS C., "Evolutionary multi-objective feature selection and ROC analysis with application to industrial machinery fault diagnosis", *Chapter in Evolutionary Methods for Design Optimisation and Control, CIMNE, Barcelona*, 2002.

[ENG 06] ENGELBRECHT A.P., *Fundamentals of computational swarm intelligence*, John Wiley & Sons, New York, 2006.

[EST 96] ESTER M., KRIEGEL H., SANDER J. *et al.*, "A density-based algorithm for discovering clusters in large spatial databases with noise", *Proceedings of the Second International Conference on Knowledge Discovery and Data Mining (KDD-96), Portland, Oregon, USA*, pp. 226–231, 1996.

[FAH 14] FAHAD A., ALSHATRI N., TARI Z. *et al.*, "A survey of clustering algorithms for Big Data: taxonomy and empirical analysis", *Transactions on Emerging Topics in Computing, IEEE* , vol. 2, no. 3, pp. 267–279, September 2014.

[FAR 02] FARHANG-MEHR A., AZARM S., "Diversity assessment of Pareto optimal solution sets: an entropy approach", *Proceedings of the 2002 Congress on Evolutionary Computation*, IEEE, pp. 723–728, 2002.

[FEO 95] FEO T.A., RESENDE M.G., "Greedy randomized adaptive search procedures", *Journal of Global Optimization*, Springer, vol. 6, no. 2, pp. 109–133, 1995.

[FER 13] FERRUCCI F., KECHADI M., SALZA P. *et al.*, "A Framework for Genetic Algorithms Based on Hadoop", *arXiv preprint arXiv:1312.0086*, 2013.

[FER 15] FERRUCCI F., SALZA P., KECHADI M.-T. *et al.*, "A parallel genetic algorithms framework based on Hadoop MapReduce", *Proceedings of the 30th Annual ACM Symposium on Applied Computing*, SAC '15, New York, NY, USA, ACM, pp. 1664–1667, 2015.

[FIS 15] FISSET B., DHAENENS C., JOURDAN L., "MO-Mine_clust: a framework for multi-objective clustering", *Learning and Intelligent Optimization - 9th International Conference, LION 9, Lille, France, January 12–15, 2015. Revised Selected Papers*, pp. 293–305, 2015.

[FOG 66] FOGEL L.J., OWENS A.J., WALSH M.J., *Artificial intelligence through simulated evolution*, John Wiley, New York, 1966.

[FON 93] FONSECA C.M., FLEMING P.J., "Genetic algorithms for multi-objective optimization: formulation discussion and generalization", *ICGA*, Citeseer, vol. 93, pp. 416–423, 1993.

[FOR 07] FORMATO R.A., "Central force optimization: a new metaheuristic with applications in applied electromagnetics", *Progress In Electromagnetics Research*, EMW Publishing, vol. 77, pp. 425–491, 2007.

[FRA 15] FRANZ W., THULASIRAMAN P., THULASIRAM R.K., "Exploration/exploitation of a hybrid-enhanced MPSO-GA algorithm on a fused CPU-GPU architecture", *Concurrency and Computation: Practice and Experience*, vol. 27, no. 4, pp. 973–993, 2015.

[FRE 99] FREITAS A.A., "On rule interestingness measures", *Knowledge-Based Systems*, Elsevier, vol. 12, no. 5, pp. 309–315, 1999.

[FRE 04] FREITAS A.A., "A critical review of multi-objective optimization in data mining: a position paper", *ACM SIGKDD Explorations Newsletter*, ACM, vol. 6, no. 2, pp. 77–86, 2004.

[FRE 08] FREITAS A.A., "A review of evolutionary algorithms for data mining", *Soft Computing for Knowledge Discovery and Data Mining*, Springer, pp. 79–111, 2008.

[FRE 13] FREITAS A.A., *Data mining and knowledge discovery with evolutionary algorithms*, Springer Science & Business Media, Berlin, 2013.

[FRI 37] FRIEDMAN M., "The use of ranks to avoid the assumption of normality implicit in the analysis of variance", *Journal of the American Statistical Association*, Taylor and Francis, vol. 32, no. 200, pp. 675–701, 1937.

[FRI 05] FRIEDRICHS F., IGEL C., "Evolutionary tuning of multiple SVM parameters", *Neurocomputing*, Elsevier, vol. 64, pp. 107–117, 2005.

[GAG 06] GAGNÉ C., PARIZEAU M., "Genicity in evolutionary computation software tools: principles and case-study", *International Journal on Artificial Intelligence Tools*, World Scientific, vol. 15, no. 02, pp. 173–194, 2006.

[GAN 14] GANGHISHETTI P., VADLAMANI R., "Association rule mining via evolutionary multi-objective optimization", *Multi-disciplinary Trends in Artificial Intelligence*, Springer, pp. 35–46, 2014.

[GAO 16] GAO W., "Improved ant colony clustering algorithm and its performance study", *Computational Intelligence and Neuroscience*, vol. 2016, Article ID 4835932, p. 14, 2016.

[GAR 08] GARCIA S., HERRERA F., SHAWE-TAYLOR J., "An extension on 'statistical comparisons of classifiers over multiple data sets' for all pairwise comparisons", *Journal of Machine Learning Research*, pp. 2677–2694, 2008.

[GAR 09a] GARCÍA-NIETO J., ALBA E., JOURDAN L. *et al.*, "Sensitivity and specificity based multiobjective approach for feature selection: application to cancer diagnosis", *Inf. Process. Lett.*, Elsevier, vol. 109, pp. 887–896, July 2009.

[GAR 09b] GARCIA-NIETO J., ALBA E., APOLLONI J., "Hybrid DE-SVM approach for feature selection: application to gene expression data sets", *Logistics and Industrial Informatics, LINDI, 2nd International*, IEEE, pp. 1–6, 2009.

[GAR 12] GARCÍA PIQUER Á., Facing-up challenges of multi-objective clustering based on evolutionary algorithms: representations, scalability and retrieval solutions, PhD thesis, Universitat Ramon Llull, 2012.

[GEN 06] GENG L., HAMILTON H., "Interestingness measures for data mining: a survey", *ACM Computing Surveys (CSUR)*, vol. 38, no. 3, 2006.

[GEN 10] GENDREAU M., POTVIN J.-Y., *Handbook of metaheuristics*, Springer, vol. 2, 2010.

[GHO 04] GHOSH A., NATH B., "Multi-objective rule mining using genetic algorithms", *Information Sciences*, Elsevier, vol. 163, no. 1, pp. 123–133, 2004.

[GHO 08] GHOSH A., HALDER A., KOTHARI M. *et al.*, "Aggregation pheromone density based data clustering", *Information Sciences*, vol. 178, no. 13, pp. 2816–2831, 2008.

[GIL 90] GILLIES D., "The turing-good weight of evidence function and popper's measure of the severity of a test", *British Journal for the Philosophy of Science*, Taylor & Francis, vol. 41, no. 1, pp. 143–146, 1990.

[GLO 77] GLOVER F., "Heuristics for integer programming using surrogate constraints", *Decision Sciences*, vol. 8, no. 1, pp. 156–166, 1977.

[GLO 89] GLOVER F., "Tabu search-part I", *ORSA Journal on Computing*, INFORMS, vol. 1, no. 3, pp. 190–206, 1989.

[GLO 98] GLOVER F., "A template for scatter search and path relinking", 3rd *European Conference on Artificial Evolution*, Springer, pp. 1–51, 1998.

[GLO 03] GLOVER F., KOCHENBERGER G.A., *Handbook of metaheuristics*, Springer Science & Business Media, Berlin, 2003.

[GOL 88] GOLDBERG D.E., HOLLAND J.H., "Genetic algorithms and machine learning", *Machine learning*, Springer, vol. 3, no. 2, pp. 95–99, 1988.

[GOL 89] GOLBERG D.E., "Genetic algorithms in search, optimization and machine learning", *Addion Wesley*, vol. 1989, 1989.

[GON 12] GONG M., MA L., ZHANG Q. *et al.*, "Community detection in networks by using multi-objective evolutionary algorithm with decomposition", *Physica A: Statistical Mechanics and its Applications*, vol. 391, no. 15, pp. 4050–4060, 2012.

[GOO 09] GOODARZI M., FREITAS M.P., JENSEN R., "Ant colony optimization as a feature selection method in the QSAR modeling of anti-HIV-1 activities of 3-(3, 5-dimethylbenzyl) uracil derivatives using MLR, PLS and SVM regressions", *Chemometrics and Intelligent Laboratory Systems*, Elsevier, vol. 98, no. 2, pp. 123–129, 2009.

[GRA 98] GRAY H.F., MAXWELL R.J., MARTÍNEZ-PÉREZ I. *et al.*, "Genetic programming for classification and feature selection: analysis of 1H nuclear magnetic resonance spectra from human brain tumour biopsies", *NMR in Biomedicine*, Wiley Online Library, vol. 11, nos 4–5, pp. 217–224, 1998.

[GRA 02] GRABUSTS P., BORISOV A., "Using grid-clustering methods in data classification", *International Conference on Parallel Computing in Electrical Engineering (PARELEC 2002), Warsaw, Poland*, p. 425, 2002.

[GRE 12] GREEN R.C., WANG L., ALAM M., "Training neural networks using central force optimization and particle swarm optimization: insights and comparisons", *Expert Systems with Applications*, Elsevier, vol. 39, no. 1, pp. 555–563, 2012.

[GUY 03] GUYON I., ELISSEEFF A., "An introduction to variable and feature selection", *The Journal of Machine Learning Research*, vol. 3, pp. 1157–1182, 2003.

[HAL 09] HALL M., FRANK E., HOLMES G. *et al.*, "The WEKA data mining software: an update", *SIGKDD Explorations*, vol. 11, no. 1, 2009.

[HAM 07] HAMDANI T.M., WON J.-M., ALIMI A.M. *et al.*, "*Adaptive and natural computing algorithms: Proceedings of 8th International Conference, Part I, ICANNGA 2007, Warsaw, Poland*, ", Springer, Chapter Multi-objective Feature Selection with NSGA II, pp. 240–247, 2007.

[HAM 13] HAMON J., Combinatorial optimization for variable selection in high dimensional regression: application in animal genetic, Thesis, University of Science and Technology, Lille, November 2013.

[HAN 78] HANSEN P., DELATTRE M., "Complete-link cluster analysis by graph coloring", *Journal of the American Statistical Association*, Taylor and Francis Group, vol. 73, no. 362, pp. 397–403, 1978.

[HAN 04] HANDL J., KNOWLES J., "Evolutionary multi-objective clustering", *In Proceedings of the 8th International Conference on Parallel Problem Solving from Nature*, Springer, pp. 1081–1091, 2004.

[HAN 05a] HAN J., *Data Mining: Concepts and Techniques*, Morgan Kaufmann Publishers Inc., San Francisco, 2005.

[HAN 05b] HANDL J., KNOWLES J., KELL D., "Computational cluster validation in post-genomic data analysis", *Bioinformatics*, vol. 21, no. 15, pp. 3201–3212, 2005.

[HAN 06] HANDL J., KNOWLES J., DORIGO M., "Ant-based clustering and topographic mapping", *Artificial Life*, vol. 12, no. 1, pp. 35–61, 2006.

[HAN 07a] HANDL J., KNOWLES J.D., "An evolutionary approach to multi-objective clustering", *IEEE Trans. Evolutionary Computation*, vol. 11, no. 1, pp. 56–76, 2007.

[HAN 07b] HANDL J., MEYER B., "Ant-based and swarm-based clustering", *Swarm Intelligence*, vol. 1, no. 2, pp. 95–113, 2007.

[HAN 07c] HANS C., DOBRA A., WEST M., "Shotgun stochastic search for "large p" regression", *Journal of the American Statistical Association*, 2007.

[HAN 12] HANDL J., KNOWLES J., "Clustering criteria in multi-objective data clustering", COELLO C., CUTELLO V., DEB K. *et al.* (eds), *Parallel Problem Solving from Nature – PPSN XII*, vol. 7492 of Lecture Notes in Computer Science, Springer, pp. 32–41, 2012.

[HED 08] HEDAR A.-R., WANG J., FUKUSHIMA M., "Tabu search for attribute reduction in rough set theory", *Soft Computing*, Springer, vol. 12, no. 9, pp. 909–918, 2008.

[HER 94] HERTZ A., JAUMARD B., RIBEIRO C. *et al.*, "A multi-criteria Tabu search approach to cell formation problems in group technology with multiple objectives", *Revue française d'automatique, d'informatique et de recherche opérationnelle. Recherche opérationnelle*, vol. 28, no. 3, pp. 303–328, 1994.

[HER 07] HERNANDEZ J., DUVAL B., HAO J., "A genetic embedded approach for gene selection and classification of microarray data", *Proceedings of the 5th European conference on Evolutionary computation, machine learning and data mining in bioinformatics*, EvoBIO'07, Springer-Verlag, pp. 90–101, 2007.

[HIL 86] HILLIS W.D., STEELE JR. G.L., "Data parallel algorithms", *Commun. ACM*, ACM, vol. 29, no. 12, pp. 1170–1183, December 1986.

[HIL 90] HILLIS W.D., "Co-evolving parasites improve simulated evolution as an optimization procedure", *Physica D: Nonlinear Phenomena*, Elsevier, vol. 42, no. 1, pp. 228–234, 1990.

[HIL 13] HILDERMAN R., HAMILTON H.J., *Knowledge discovery and measures of interest*, Springer Science & Business Media, vol. 638, 2013.

[HOL 75] HOLLAND J., *Adaptation in natural and artificial systems*, University of Michigan Press, Ann Arbor, MI, 1975.

[HOL 05] HOLDEN N., FREITAS A.A., "A hybrid particle swarm/ant colony algorithm for the classification of hierarchical biological data", *SIS*, pp. 100–107, 2005.

[HOL 08] HOLDEN N., FREITAS A.A., "A hybrid PSO/ACO algorithm for discovering classification rules in data mining", *J. Artif. Evol. App.*, Hindawi Publishing Corp., vol. 2008, pp. 2:1–2:11, 2008.

[HRU 04] HRUSCHKA E., CAMPELLO R., DE CASTRO L., "Improving the efficiency of a clustering genetic algorithm", vol. 3315, pp. 861–870, 2004.

[HRU 09] HRUSCHKA E., CAMPELLO R., FREITAS A. *et al.*, "A survey of evolutionary algorithms for clustering", *IEEE Transactions on Systems, Man and Cybernetics Part C: Applications and Reviews*, vol. 39, no. 2, pp. 133–155, 2009.

[HU 07] HU J., YANG-LI X., "Association rules mining using multi-objective coevolutionary algorithm", *International Conference on Computational Intelligence and Security Workshops(CISW)*, IEEE, pp. 405–408, 2007.

[HU 14] HU W.-C., KAABOUCH N., *Big Data Management, Technologies and Applications*, Advances in Data Mining and Database Management, IGI Global, 2014.

[HUA 08] HUANG D.-S., DU J.-X., "A constructive hybrid structure optimization methodology for radial basis probabilistic neural networks", *IEEE Transactions on Neural Networks*, IEEE, vol. 19, no. 12, pp. 2099–2115, 2008.

[HUA 13] HUANG H.-C., "FPGA-based parallel metaheuristic PSO algorithm and its application to global path planning for autonomous robot navigation", *Journal of Intelligent and Robotic Systems*, vol. 76, no. 3, pp. 475–488, 2013.

[HUE 06] HUERTA E., DUVAL B., HAO J., "A hybrid GA/SVM approach for gene selection and classification of microarray data", *Evoworkshops 2006*, LNCS, vol. 3907, pp. 34–44, 2006.

[HUM 13] HUMEAU J., LIEFOOGHE A., TALBI E.-G. *et al.*, "ParadisEO-MO: from fitness landscape analysis to efficient local search algorithms", *Journal of Heuristics*, Springervol. 19, no. 6, pp. 881–915, 2013.

[IBM 16a] IBM, "The four V's of Big Data",   available at: www.ibmbigdatahub.com/infographic/four-vs-big-data, 2016.

[IBM 16b] IBM, "What is Big Data?", available at: https://www-01.ibm.com/software/data/bigdata/what-is-big-data.html, 2016.

[IGE 05] IGEL C., WIEGAND S., FRIEDRICHS F., "Evolutionary optimization of neural systems: the use of strategy adaptation", *Trends and applications in constructive approximation*, Springer, pp. 103–123, 2005.

[IGL 05] DE LA IGLESIA B., REYNOLDS A., RAYWARD-SMITH V.J., "Developments on a multi-objective metaheuristic (MOMH) algorithm for finding interesting sets of classification rules", *Evolutionary Multi-Criterion Optimization*, Springer, pp. 826–840, 2005.

[IGL 06] DE LA IGLESIA B., RICHARDS G., PHILPOTT M.S. *et al.*, "The application and effectiveness of a multi-objective metaheuristic algorithm for partial classification", *European Journal of Operational Research*, Elsevier, vol. 169, no. 3, pp. 898–917, 2006.

[IMA 80] IMAN R.L., DAVENPORT J.M., "Approximations of the critical region of the fbietkan statistic", *Communications in Statistics-Theory and Methods*, Taylor and Francis, vol. 9, no. 6, pp. 571–595, 1980.

[ISH 98] ISHIBUCHI H., MURATA T., "A multi-objective genetic local search algorithm and its application to flowshop scheduling", *IEEE Transactions on Systems, Man and Cybernetics, Part C: Applications and Reviews*, IEEE, vol. 28, no. 3, pp. 392–403, 1998.

[JAC 13a] JACQUES J., Classification sur données médicales à l'aide de méthodes d'optimisation et de datamining, appliquée au pré-screening dans les essais cliniques, PhD thesis, Lille University of Science and Technology, Lille I, 2013.

[JAC 13b] JACQUES J., TAILLARD J., DELERUE D. *et al.*, "The benefits of using multi-objectivization for mining pittsburgh partial classification rules in imbalanced and discrete data", *Proceedings of the 15th annual conference on Genetic and evolutionary computation*, ACM, pp. 543–550, 2013.

[JAC 15] JACQUES J., TAILLARD J., DELERUE D. *et al.*, "Conception of a dominance-based multi-objective local search in the context of classification rule mining in large and imbalanced data sets", *Applied Soft Computing*, Elsevier, vol. 34, pp. 705–720, 2015.

[JAG 14] JAGADISH H., GEHRKE J., LABRINIDIS A. *et al.*, "Big Data and its technical challenges", *Communications of the ACM*, ACM, vol. 57, no. 7, pp. 86–94, 2014.

[JAI 88] JAIN A.K., DUBES R.C., *Algorithms for clustering data*, Prentice Hall, Upper Saddle River, 1988.

[JEN 06] JENSEN R., "Performing feature selection with ACO", *Swarm Intelligence in Data Mining*, Springer, pp. 45–73, 2006.

[JES 11] DEL JESUS M.J., GAMEZ J.A., GONZALEZ P. *et al.*, "On the discovery of association rules by means of evolutionary algorithms", *Wiley Interdisciplinary Reviews: Data Mining and Knowledge Discovery*, Wiley Online Library, vol. 1, no. 5, pp. 397–415, 2011.

[JIR 05] JIRAPECH-UMPAI T., AITKEN S., "Feature selection and classification for microarray data analysis: evolutionary methods for identifying predictive genes", *BMC bioinformatics*, vol. 6, no. 1, p. 148, 2005.

[JOS 16] JOSÉ-GARCÍA A., GOMEZ-FLORES W., "Automatic clustering using nature-inspired metaheuristics: A survey", *Applied Soft Computing Journal*, vol. 41, pp. 192–213, 2016.

[JOU 01] JOURDAN L., DHAENENS C., TALBI E.-G., "A genetic algorithm for feature selection in data mining for genetics", *Proceedings of the 4th Metaheuristics International (MIC, 2001)*, pp. 29–34, 2001.

[JOU 04] JOURDAN L., DHAENENS C., TALBI E.-G., "Linkage disequilibrium study with a parallel adaptive GA", *International Journal of Foundations of Computer Science*, 2004.

[JUL 05] JULIUSDOTTIR T., CORNE D., KEEDWELL E. *et al.*, "Two-phase EA/k-NN for feature selection and classification in cancer microarray datasets", *Proceedings of the 2005 IEEE Symposium on Computational Intelligence in Bioinformatics and Computational Biology, CIBCB 2005, USA, November 14 – 15, 2005*, pp. 1–8, 2005.

[KAB 12] KABIR M.M., SHAHJAHAN M., MURASE K., "A new hybrid ant colony optimization algorithm for feature selection", *Expert Systems with Applications*, Elsevier, vol. 39, no. 3, pp. 3747–3763, 2012.

[KAL 10] KALLES D., PAPAGELIS A., "Lossless fitness inheritance in genetic algorithms for decision trees", *Soft Computing*, Springer-Verlag, vol. 14, no. 9, pp. 973–993, 2010.

[KAN 07] KANAN H.R., FAEZ K., TAHERI S.M., "Feature selection using ant colony optimization (ACO): a new method and comparative study in the application of face recognition system", *Theoretical Aspects and Applications Advances in Data Mining*, Springer, pp. 63–76, 2007.

[KAN 08] KANAN H.R., FAEZ K., "An improved feature selection method based on ant colony optimization (ACO) evaluated on face recognition system", *Applied Mathematics and Computation*, Elsevier, vol. 205, no. 2, pp. 716–725, 2008.

[KAP 05] KAPETANIOS G., Variable selection using non-standard optimisation of information criteria, Report , Working Paper, Department of Economics, Queen Mary, University of London, 2005.

[KAR 90] KARP A.H., FLATT H.P., "Measuring parallel processor performance", *Communications of the ACM*, ACM, vol. 33, no. 5, pp. 539–543, 1990.

[KAR 06] KARASOZEN B., RUBINOV A., WEBER G.-W., "Optimization in data mining", *European Journal of Operational Research*, vol. 173, no. 3, pp. 701–704, 2006.

[KAR 09] KARABOGA D., AKAY B., "A survey: algorithms simulating bee swarm intelligence", *Artificial Intelligence Review*, Kluwer Academic Publishers, vol. 31, nos 1–4, pp. 61–85, 2009.

[KAU 87] KAUFMAN L., ROUSSEEUW P., Clustering by Means of Medoids, Reports of the Faculty of Mathematics and Informatics, Faculty of Mathematics and Informatics, 1987.

[KAY 05] KAYA M., ALHAJJ R., "Genetic algorithm based framework for mining fuzzy association rules", *Fuzzy Sets and Systems*, Elsevier, vol. 152, no. 3, pp. 587–601, 2005.

[KAY 06] KAYA M., "Multi-objective genetic algorithm based approaches for mining optimized fuzzy association rules", *Soft Computing*, Springer, vol. 10, no. 7, pp. 578–586, 2006.

[KEN 95] KENNEDY J., EBERHART R., "Particle swarm optimization", *IEEE International Conference on Neural Networks*, vol. 1, pp. 1942–1948, 1995.

[KEN 10] KENNEDY J., "Particle swarm optimization", *Encyclopedia of Machine Learning*, Springer, pp. 760–766, 2010.

[KHA 04] KHABZAOUI M., DHAENENS C., TALBI E.-G., "A multicriteria genetic algorithm to analyze microarray data", *Congress on Evolutionary Computation,* vol. 2, pp. 1874–1881, 2004.

[KHA 05] KHABZAOUI M., DHAENENS C., TALBI E.-G., "Parallel genetic algorithms for multi-objective rule mining", *The 6th MIC2005*, 2005.

[KHA 08] KHABZAOUI M., DHAENENS C., TALBI E.-G., "Combining evolutionary algorithms and exact approaches for multi-objective knowledge discovery", *RAIRO-Operations Research-Recherche Opérationnelle*, vol. 42, no. 1, pp. 69–83, 2008.

[KHA 12] KHAN K., SAHAI A., "A comparison of BA, GA, PSO, BP and LM for training feed forward neural networks in e-learning context", *International Journal of Intelligent Systems and Applications*, Modern Education and Computer Science Press, vol. 4, no. 7, p. 23, 2012.

[KIM 02] KIM Y., STREET W., MENCZER F., "*Data mining: opportunities and challenges*", Idea Group, Chapter Feature selection in data mining, pp. 80–105, 2002.

[KIR 83] KIRKPATRICK S., GELATT C.D., VECCHI M.P., "Optimization by simulated annealing", *Science*, World Scientific, vol. 220, no. 4598, pp. 671–680, 1983.

[KIR 92] KIRA K., RENDELL L.A., "A practical approach to feature selection", *Proceedings of the 9th international workshop on Machine learning*, pp. 249–256, 1992.

[KNO 00] KNOWLES J.D., CORNE D.W., "Approximating the non-dominated front using the Pareto archived evolution strategy", *Evolutionary computation*, MIT Press, vol. 8, no. 2, pp. 149–172, 2000.

[KNO 02] KNOWLES J., CORNE D., "On metrics for comparing non-dominated sets", *Proceedings of the 2002 Congress on Evolutionary Computation*, IEEE, vol. 1, pp. 711–716, 2002.

[KOH 97] KOHAVI R., JOHN G.H., "Wrappers for feature subset selection", *Artificial intelligence*, Elsevier, vol. 97, no. 1, pp. 273–324, 1997.

[KOZ 92] KOZA J.R., *Genetic programming: on the programming of computers by means of natural selection*, MIT press, Cambridge, MA, USA, vol. 1, 1992.

[KRÖ 14] KRÖMER P., PLATO J., SNÁEL V., "Nature-inspired metaheuristics on modern GPUs: state-of-the-art and brief survey of selected algorithms", *Int. J. Parallel Program.*, Kluwer Academic Publishers, vol. 42, no. 5, pp. 681–709, October 2014.

[KRI 99] KRISHNA K., MURTY M., "Genetic K-means algorithm", *IEEE Transactions on Systems, Man, and Cybernetics, Part B: Cybernetics*, vol. 29, no. 3, pp. 433–439, 1999.

[KRI 09] KRIEGEL H.-P., KRÖGER P., ZIMEK A., "Clustering high-dimensional data: a survey on subspace clustering, pattern-based clustering and correlation clustering", *ACM Trans. Knowl. Discov. Data*, ACM, vol. 3, pp. 1:1–1:58, 2009.

[KRU 52] KRUSKAL W.H., WALLIS W.A., "Use of ranks in one-criterion variance analysis", *Journal of the American statistical Association*, Taylor & Francis, vol. 47, no. 260, pp. 583–621, 1952.

[KUR 13] KURADA R.R., PAVAN D.K.K., RAO D.A., "A preliminary survey on optimized multi-objective metaheuristic methods for data clustering using evolutionary approaches", *arXiv preprint arXiv:1312.2366*, 2013.

[LAI 09] LAI C.-C., CHANG C.-Y., "A hierarchical evolutionary algorithm for automatic medical image segmentation", *Expert Systems with Applications*, vol. 36, no. 1, pp. 248–259, 2009.

[LAN 01] LANEY D., "3D data management: controlling data volume, velocity and variety", *Gartner Retrieved*, vol. 6, 2001.

[LAN 15] LANDSET S., KHOSHGOFTAAR T.M., RICHTER A.N., *et al.*, "A survey of open source tools for machine learning with big data in the Hadoop ecosystem", *Journal of Big Data*, Springer, vol. 2, no. 1, pp. 1–36, 2015.

[LAR 14] LAROSE D.T., *Discovering knowledge in data: an introduction to data mining*, John Wiley & Sons, 2014.

[LES 16] LESUEUR D., "Five reasons healthcare data is unique and difficult to measure", available at: https://www.healthcatalyst.com/5-reasons-healthcare-data-is-difficult-to-measure/, 2016.

[LEU 12] LEUNG S., TANG Y., WONG W.K., "A hybrid particle swarm optimization and its application in neural networks", *Expert Systems with Applications*, Elsevier, vol. 39, no. 1, pp. 395–405, 2012.

[LIE 08] LIEFOOGHE A., JOURDAN L., BASSEUR M. *et al.*, "Metaheuristics for the bi-objective ring star problem", *Evolutionary Computation in Combinatorial Optimization*, Springer, pp. 206–217, 2008.

[LIE 11] LIEFOOGHE A., JOURDAN L., TALBI E., "A software framework based on a conceptual unified model for evolutionary multi-objective optimization: ParadisEO-MOEO", *European Journal of Operational Research*, vol. 209, no. 2, pp. 104–112, 2011.

[LIE 12] LIEFOOGHE A., HUMEAU J., MESMOUDI S. *et al.*, "On dominance-based multiobjective local search: design, implementation and experimental analysis on scheduling and traveling salesman problems", *Journal of Heuristics*, Springer, vol. 18, no. 2, pp. 317–352, 2012.

[LIU 01] LIU J., IBA H., ISHIZUKA M., "Selecting informative genes with parallel genetic algorithms in tissue classification", *Genome Informatics Series*, pp. 14–23, 2001.

[LIU 02] LIU J., IBA H., "Selecting informative genes using a multi-objective evolutionary algorithm", *Proceedings of the 2002 Congress on Evolutionary Computation*, IEEE, vol. 1, pp. 297–302, 2002.

[LIU 07] LIU H., MOTODA H., *Computational Methods of Feature Selection* (Chapman & Hall/Crc Data Mining and Knowledge Discovery Series), Chapman & Hall/CRC, London, 2007.

[LIU 11] LIU Y., WANG G., CHEN H. *et al.*, "An improved particle swarm optimization for feature selection", *Journal of Bionic Engineering*, Elsevier, vol. 8, no. 2, pp. 191–200, 2011.

[LON 07] LONG N., GIANOLA D., ROSA G. *et al.*, "Machine learning classification procedure for selecting SNPs in genomic selection: application to early mortality in broilers", *Journal of animal breeding and genetics*, Wiley Online Library, vol. 124, no. 6, pp. 377–389, 2007.

[LOP 06] LÓPEZ F.G., TORRES M.G., BATISTA B.M. *et al.*, "Solving feature subset selection problem by a parallel scatter search", *European Journal of Operational Research*, Elsevier, vol. 169, no. 2, pp. 477–489, 2006.

[LOU 10] LOURENÇO H.R., MARTIN O.C., STÜTZLE T., "Iterated local search: framework and applications", *Handbook of Metaheuristics*, Springer, pp. 363–397, 2010.

[LOZ 04] LOZANO M., HERRERA F., KRASNOGOR N. *et al.*, "Real-coded memetic algorithms with crossover hill-climbing", *Evolutionary Computation*, MIT Press, vol. 12, no. 3, pp. 273–302, 2004.

[LUO 13] LUONG T.V., MELAB N., TALBI E., "GPU computing for parallel local search metaheuristic algorithms", *IEEE Transactions on Computers*, IEEE Computer Society, vol. 62, no. 1, pp. 173–185, 2013.

[LUQ 11] LUQUE G., ALBA E., *Parallel Genetic Algorithms*, vol. 367 of Studies in Computational Intelligence, Springer, New York, 2011.

[MAC 67] MACQUEEN J., "Some methods for classification and analysis of multivariate observations", *Proc. 5th Berkeley Symp. Math. Stat. Probab.*, Univ. Calif., 1967.

[MAI 07] MAIMON O., ROKACH L., *Soft computing for knowledge discovery and data mining*, Springer Science and Business Media, Berlin, 2007.

[MAI 10] MAIMON O., ROKACH L., *Data mining and knowledge discovery handbook – 2nd edition*, Springer, New York, 2010.

[MAN 47] MANN H.B., WHITNEY D.R., "On a test of whether one of two random variables is stochastically larger than the other", *The annals of mathematical statistics*, JSTOR, pp. 50–60, 1947.

[MAN 15] MANTOVANI R.G., ROSSI A.L., VANSCHOREN J. *et al.*, "Effectiveness of random search in SVM hyper-parameter tuning", *International Joint Conference on Neural Networks*, IEEE, pp. 1–8, 2015.

[MAR 06] MARTÍ R., LAGUNA M., GLOVER F., "Principles of scatter search", *European Journal of Operational Research*, Elsevier, vol. 169, no. 2, pp. 359–372, 2006.

[MAR 08] MARINAKIS Y., MARINAKI M., DOUMPOS M. *et al.*, "Optimization of nearest neighbor classifiers via metaheuristic algorithms for credit risk assessment", *Journal of Global Optimization*, Springer US, vol. 42, no. 2, pp. 279–293, 2008.

[MAR 11] MARTÍNEZ-BALLESTEROS M., MARTÍNEZ-ÁLVAREZ F., TRONCOSO A. *et al.*, "An evolutionary algorithm to discover quantitative association rules in multidimensional time series", *Soft Computing*, Springer, vol. 15, no. 10, pp. 2065–2084, 2011.

[MAR 14] MARTÍN D., ROSETE A., ALCALÁ-FDEZ J. *et al.*, "QAR-CIP-NSGA-II: A new multi-objective evolutionary algorithm to mine quantitative association rules", *Information Sciences*, Elsevier, vol. 258, pp. 1–28, 2014.

[MAR 16] MARTÍNEZ-BALLESTEROS M., TRONCOSO A., MARTÍNEZ-ÁLVAREZ F. *et al.*, "Obtaining optimal quality measures for quantitative association rules", *Neurocomputing*, Elsevier, vol. 176, pp. 36–47, 2016.

[MAT 11] MATTHEWS S.G., GONGORA M.A., HOPGOOD A.A., "Evolving temporal fuzzy association rules from quantitative data with a multi-objective evolutionary algorithm", *Hybrid Artificial Intelligent Systems*, Springer, pp. 198–205, 2011.

[MAU 00] MAULIK U., BANDYOPADHYAY S., "Genetic algorithm-based clustering technique", *Pattern Recognition*, vol. 33, no. 9, pp. 1455–1465, 2000.

[MEI 06] MEIRI R., ZAHAVI J., "Using simulated annealing to optimize the feature selection problem in marketing applications", *European Journal of Operational Research*, Elsevier, vol. 171, no. 3, pp. 842–858, Elsevier, 2006.

[MEI 10] MEISEL S., MATTFELD D., "Synergies of operations research and data mining", *European Journal of Operational Research*, vol. 206, no. 1, pp. 1–10, 2010.

[MEL 13] MELAB N., LUONG T.V., BOUFARAS K. *et al.*, "ParadisEO-MO-GPU: a framework for parallel GPU-based local search metaheuristics", *ACM GECCO'2013*, Amsterdam, Netherlands, July 2013.

[MEN 13] MENTIS A.S., YILMAZ L., "Adapting a natural system simulation model to a general-purpose metaheuristic: toward engineering emergent distributed decision-making", *Proceedings of the 2013 Summer Computer Simulation Conference*, Vista, CA, Society for Modeling; Simulation International, pp. 44:1–44:6, 2013.

[MEU 00] MEUNIER H., TALBI E.-G., REININGER P., "A multiobjective genetic algorithm for radio network optimization", *Proceedings of the 2000 Congress on Evolutionary Computation*, vol. 1, IEEE, pp. 317–324, 2000.

[MIK 15] MIKE2.0, "Big Data Definition", available at: http://mike2.openmethodology.org/ wiki/Big_Data_Definition, 2015.

[MIR 96] MIRKIN B., *Mathematical Classification and Clustering*,   Kluwer Academic Publishers, 1996.

[MIT 02] MITRA S., PAL S., MITRA P., "Data mining in soft computing framework: a survey", *IEEE Transactions on Neural Networks*, vol. 13, no. 1, pp. 3–14, January 2002.

[MLA 97] MLADENOVI N., HANSEN P., "Variable neighborhood search", *Computers and Operations Research*, Elsevier, vol. 24, no. 11, pp. 1097–1100, 1997.

[MOH 08] MOHAMADI H., HABIBI J., ABADEH M.S. *et al.*, "Data mining with a simulated annealing based fuzzy classification system", *Pattern Recognition*, vol. 41, no. 5, pp. 1824–1833, 2008.

[MOO 10] MOORE J.H., ASSELBERGS F.W., WILLIAMS S.M., "Bioinformatics challenges for genome-wide association studies", *Bioinformatics*, vol. 26, no. 4, pp. 445–455, Oxford University Press, 2010.

[MUK 07] MUKHOPADHYAY A., MAULIK U., "Multi-objective approach to categorical data clustering", *IEEE Congress on Evolutionary Computation*, pp. 1296–1303, September 2007.

[MUK 09] MUKHOPADHYAY A., MAULIK U., BANDYOPADHYAY S., "Multi-objective genetic algorithm-based fuzzy clustering of categorical attributes", *IEEE Trans. Evolutionary Computation*, vol. 13, no. 5, pp. 991–1005, 2009.

[MUK 11] MUKHOPADHYAY A., MAULIK U., "A multi-objective approach to {MR} brain image segmentation", *Applied Soft Computing*, vol. 11, no. 1, pp. 872–880, 2011.

[MUK 14a] MUKHOPADHYAY A., MAULIK U., BANDYOPADHYAY S. *et al.*, "A survey of multi-objective evolutionary algorithms for data mining: Part II", *IEEE Transactions on Evolutionary Computation*, IEEE, vol. 18, no. 1, pp. 20–35, 2014.

[MUK 14b] MUKHOPADHYAY A., MAULIK U., BANDYOPADHYAY S. *et al.*, "A survey of multiobjective evolutionary algorithms for data mining: Part I", *IEEE Transactions on Evolutionary Computation*, IEEE, vol. 18, no. 1, pp. 4–19, 2014.

[MUK 15] MUKHOPADHYAY A., MAULIK U., BANDYOPADHYAY S., "A survey of multi-objective evolutionary clustering", *ACM Comput. Surv.*, vol. 47, no. 4, p. 61, 2015.

[MUN 06] MUNI D., PAL N., DAS J., "Genetic programming for simultaneous feature selection and classifier design", *IEEE Transactions on Systems, Man and Cybernetics, Part B: Cybernetics*, vol. 36, no. 1, pp. 106–117, February 2006.

[MUR 96] MURTHY C., CHOWDHURY N., "In search of optimal clusters using genetic algorithms", *Pattern Recognition Letters*, vol. 17, no. 8, pp. 825–832, 1996.

[NAK 12] NAKAMURA R.Y., PEREIRA L.A., COSTA K. *et al.*, "BBA: a binary bat algorithm for feature selection", *25th SIBGRAPI Conference on Graphics, Patterns and Images*, IEEE, pp. 291–297, 2012.

[NAN 14] NANDA S.J., PANDA G., "A survey on nature inspired metaheuristic algorithms for partitional clustering", *Swarm and Evolutionary Computation*, vol. 16, pp. 1–18, 2014.

[NAR 77] NARENDRA P.M., FUKUNAGA K., "A branch and bound algorithm for feature subset selection", *IEEE Trans. Comput.*, IEEE Computer Society, vol. 26, no. 9, pp. 917–922, September 1977.

[NEB 10] NEBRO A.J., DURILLO J.J., in Chapter "A study of the parallelization of the multi-objective metaheuristic MOEA/D", *Learning and Intelligent Optimization: 4th International Conference, LION 4, Venice, Italy, January 18–22, 2010*, Springer, pp. 303–317, 2010.

[NEB 15] NEBRO A.J., DURILLO J.J., VERGNE M., "Redesigning the jMetal multi-objective optimization framework", *Proceedings of the Companion Publication of the 2015 Annual Conference on Genetic and Evolutionary Computation*, GECCO Companion, ACM, pp. 1093–1100, New York, USA, 2015.

[NEM 09] NEMATI S., BASIRI M.E., GHASEM-AGHAEE N. *et al.*, "A novel ACO–GA hybrid algorithm for feature selection in protein function prediction", *Expert systems with applications*, Elsevier, vol. 36, no. 10, pp. 12086–12094, 2009.

[NOC 06] NOCK R., NIELSEN F., "On weighting clustering", *IEEE Trans. Pattern Anal. Mach. Intell.*, vol. 28, no. 8, pp. 1223–1235, 2006.

[NUN 14] NUNEZ S.G., ATTOH-OKINE N., "Metaheuristics in Big Data: an approach to railway engineering", *IEEE International Conference on Big Data*, IEEE, pp. 42–47, 2014.

[OH 04] OH I., LEE J., MOON B., "Hybrid genetic algorithms for feature selection", *IEEE Transactions on Pattern Analysis and Machine Intelligence*, vol. 26, no. 11, pp. 1424–1437, November 2004.

[OHS 07] OHSAKI M., ABE H., TSUMOTO S. *et al.*, "Evaluation of rule interestingness measures in medical knowledge discovery in databases", *Artificial Intelligence in Medicine*, vol. 41, pp. 177–196, 2007.

[OLA 06] OLAFSSON S., "Introduction to operations research and data mining", *Computers and Operations Research*, vol. 33, no. 11, pp. 3067–3069, 2006.

[OLA 08] OLAFSSON S., LI X., WU S., "Operations research and data mining", *European Journal of Operational Research*, vol. 187, no. 3, pp. 1429–1448, 2008.

[OMR 06] OMRAN M.G., SALMAN A., ENGELBRECHT A.P., "Dynamic clustering using particle swarm optimization with application in image segmentation", *Pattern Anal. Appl.*, Springer-Verlag, vol. 8, no. 4, pp. 332–344, February 2006.

[OTE 08] OTERO F.E., FREITAS A.A., JOHNSON C.G., "Ant-miner: an ant colony classification algorithm to cope with continuous attributes", *Ant Colony Optimization and Swarm Intelligence*, Springer, pp. 48–59, 2008.

[OTE 12] OTERO F.E., FREITAS A.A., JOHNSON C.G., "Inducing decision trees with an ant colony optimization algorithm", *Applied Soft Computing*, Elsevier, vol. 12, no. 11, pp. 3615–3626, 2012.

[OTE 15] OTERO F.E., FREITAS A.A., "Improving the interpretability of classification rules discovered by an ant colony algorithm: extended results", *Evolutionary computation*, MIT Press, 2015.

[PAC 09] PACHECO J., CASADO S., NÚÑEZ L., "A variable selection method based on Tabu search for logistic regression models", *European Journal of Operational Research*, Elsevier, vol. 199, no. 2, pp. 506–511, 2009.

[PAL 12] PALACIOS A., GACTO M., ALCALÁ-FDEZ J., "Mining fuzzy association rules from low-quality data", *Soft Computing*, Springer-Verlag, vol. 16, no. 5, pp. 883–901, 2012.

[PAP 00] PAPAGELIS A., KALLES D., "GA tree: genetically evolved decision trees", *Proceedings of the 12th IEEE International Conference on Tools with Artificial Intelligence*, ICTAI '00, IEEE Computer Society, p. 203, Washington, DC, USA, pp. 203–206, 2000.

[PAP 04] PAPPA G.L., FREITAS A.A., KAESTNER C.A., "Multi-objective algorithms for attribute selection in data mining", *Applications of Multi-objective Evolutionary Algorithms*, World Scientific, pp. 603–626, 2004.

[PAP 09] PAPPA G.L., FREITAS A.A., "Automatically evolving rule induction algorithms tailored to the prediction of postsynaptic activity in proteins", *Intelligent Data Analysis*, IOS Press, vol. 13, no. 2, pp. 243–259, 2009.

[PAQ 04] PAQUETE L., CHIARANDINI M., STÜTZLE T., "Pareto local optimum sets in the bi-objective traveling salesman problem: an experimental study", *Metaheuristics for Multiobjective Optimisation*, Springer, pp. 177–199, 2004.

[PAR 96] PARETO V., *Cours d'économie politique*, vol. 1, F. Rouge, 1896.

[PAR 12] PAREJO J., RUIZ-CORTÉS A., LOZANO S. *et al.*, "Metaheuristic optimization frameworks: a survey and benchmarking", *Soft Computing*, Springer-Verlag, vol. 16, no. 3, pp. 527–561, 2012.

[PAS 02] PASSINO K.M., "Biomimicry of bacterial foraging for distributed optimization and control", *Control Systems, IEEE*, vol. 22, no. 3, pp. 52–67, 2002.

[PED 13] PEDEMONTE M., LUNA F., ALBA E., in Chapter "New Ideas in Parallel Metaheuristics on GPU: Systolic Genetic Search", *Massively parallel evolutionary computation on GPGPUs*, Springer, pp. 203–225, 2013.

[PEN 03] PENG S., "Molecular classification of cancer types from microarray data using the combination of genetic algorithms and support vector machines", *FEBS Letters*, vol. 555, no. 2, pp. 358–362, December 2003.

[PHU 05] PHUONG T.M., LIN Z., ALTMAN R.B., "Choosing SNPs using feature selection", *Fourth International IEEE Computer Society Computational Systems Bioinformatics Conference, CSB 2005, Stanford, CA, USA,*, pp. 301–309, August 8-11, 2005.

[PUL 08] PULKKINEN P., KOIVISTO H., "Fuzzy classifier identification using decision tree and multiobjective evolutionary algorithms", *International Journal of Approximate Reasoning*, Elsevier, vol. 48, no. 2, pp. 526–543, 2008.

[QOD 11] QODMANAN H.R., NASIRI M., MINAEI-BIDGOLI B., "Multi-objective association rule mining with genetic algorithm without specifying minimum support and minimum confidence", *Expert Systems with applications*, Elsevier, vol. 38, no. 1, pp. 288–298, 2011.

[QUI 93] QUINLAN J.R., *C4.5: programs for machine learning*, Morgan Kaufmann Publishers Inc., Burlington, 1993.

[RAG 11] RAGNARSSON R.M., HLYNUR STEF, ÅSGEIRSSON E.I., "Metaheuristics in multi-core environments", *Systems Engineering Procedia*, vol. 1, pp. 457–464, 2011.

[RAN 10] RANA S., JASOLA S., KUMAR R., "A review on particle swarm optimization algorithms and their applications to data clustering", *Artificial Intelligence Review*, vol. 35, no. 3, pp. 211–222, 2010.

[REB 13] REBENTROST P., MOHSENI M., LLOYD S., "Quantum support vector machine for big feature and Big Data classification", *arXiv preprint arXiv:1307.0471*, 2013.

[REC 65] RECHENBERG I., "Cybernetic solution path of an experimental problem", Ministry of Aviation, Royal Aircraft Establishment, 1965.

[REC 73] RECHENBERG I., "Optimierung technischer Systeme nach Prinzipien der biologischen Evolution", *Frommann-Holzboog Verlag, Stuttgart*, 1973.

[REF 09] REFAEILZADEH P., TANG L., LIU H., "Cross-validation", *Encyclopedia of Database Systems*, Springer, pp. 532–538, 2009.

[ROB 09] ROBILLIARD D., MARION V., FONLUPT C., "High performance genetic programming on GPU", *Proceedings of the 2009 workshop on Bio-inspired algorithms for distributed systems*, ACM, pp. 85–94, 2009.

[ROD 14] RODRIGUES D., PEREIRA L.A., NAKAMURA R.Y. *et al.*, "A wrapper approach for feature selection based on bat algorithm and optimum-path forest", *Expert Systems with Applications*, Elsevier, vol. 41, no. 5, pp. 2250–2258, 2014.

[ROU 87] ROUSSEEUW P.J., "Silhouettes: a graphical aid to the interpretation and validation of cluster analysis", *Journal of Computational and Applied Mathematics*, vol. 20, pp. 53–65, 1987.

[RUD 00] RUDOLPH G., AGAPIE A., Convergence properties of some multi-objective evolutionary algorithms, Univ., SFB 531, 2000.

[RUN 04] RUNARSSON T.P., SIGURDSSON S., "Asynchronous parallel evolutionary model selection for support vector machines", *Neural Information Processing-Letters and Reviews*, vol. 3, no. 3, pp. 59–68, 2004.

[SAH 11] SAHA I., MAULIK U., PLEWCZYNSKI D., "A new multi-objective technique for differential fuzzy clustering", *Applied Soft Computing*, vol. 11, no. 2, pp. 2765–2776, 2011.

[SAL 05] SALCEDO-SANZ S., XU Y., YAO X., "Metaheuristic algorithms for FPGA segmented channel routing problems with non-standard cost functions", *Genetic Programming and Evolvable Machines*, vol. 6, no. 4, pp. 359–379, 2005.

[SAL 07] SALLEB-AOUISSI A., VRAIN C., NORTET C., "QuantMiner: a genetic algorithm for mining quantitative association rules", *IJCAI*, vol. 7, 2007.

[SAL 14] SALAMA K.M., OTERO F.E., "Learning multi-tree classification models with ant colony optimization", *Proceedings international conference on evolutionary computation theory and applications (ECTA-14)*, pp. 38–48, 2014.

[SAL 15] SALAMA K.M., ABDELBAR A.M., OTERO F.E., "Investigating evaluation measures in ant colony algorithms for learning decision tree classifiers", *Computational Intelligence, 2015 IEEE Sysposium Series on*, pp. 1146–1153, 2015.

[SAN 12] SANTANDER-JIMÉNEZ S., VEGA-RODRIGUEZ M.A., GOMEZ-PULIDO J.A. *et al.*, "Evaluating the performance of a parallel multi-objective artificial bee colony algorithm for inferring phylogenies on multi-core architectures", *Parallel and Distributed Processing with Applications (ISPA), 2012 IEEE 10th International Symposium on*, IEEE, pp. 713–720, 2012.

[SAR 97] SARKAR M., YEGNANARAYANA B., KHEMANI D., "A clustering algorithm using an evolutionary programming-based approach", *Pattern Recognition Letters*, vol. 18, no. 10, pp. 975–986, 1997.

[SCH 85] SCHAFFER J.D., "Multiple objective optimization with vector evaluated genetic algorithms", *Proceedings of the 1st International Conference on Genetic Algorithms, Pittsburgh, PA, USA*, pp. 93–100, 1985.

[SHA 04] SHAH S.C., KUSIAK A., "Data mining and genetic algorithm based gene/SNP selection", *Artificial Intelligence in Medicine*, Elsevier, vol. 31, no. 3, pp. 183–196, 2004.

[SHA 06] SHAN Y., MCKAY R.I., ESSAM D. *et al.*, "A survey of probabilistic model building genetic programming", *Scalable Optimization via Probabilistic Modeling*, Springer, pp. 121–160, 2006.

[SHA 13] SHARMA A., ZAIDI A., SINGH R. *et al.*, "Optimization of SVM classifier using Firefly algorithm", *Image Information Processing (ICIIP), 2013 IEEE Second International Conference on*, IEEE, pp. 198–202, 2013.

[SHE 03] SHENOY P.D., SRINIVASA K., VENUGOPAL K. *et al.*, "Evolutionary approach for mining association rules on dynamic databases", *Advances in knowledge discovery and data mining*, Springer, pp. 325–336, 2003.

[SHE 04] SHELOKAR P., JAYARAMAN V., KULKARNI B., "An ant colony approach for clustering", *Analytica Chimica Acta*, vol. 509, no. 2, pp. 187–195, 2004.

[SHE 05] SHENOY P.D., SRINIVASA K., VENUGOPAL K. *et al.*, "Dynamic association rule mining using genetic algorithms", *Intelligent Data Analysis*, IOS Press, vol. 9, no. 5, pp. 439–453, 2005.

[SHE 08] SHEIKH R., RAGHUWANSHI M., JAISWAL A., "Genetic algorithm based clustering: a survey", pp. 314–319, 2008.

[SHI 04] SHI S.Y., SUGANTHAN P.N., "Multiclass protein fold recognition using multiobjective evolutionary algorithms", *Proceedings of the 2004 IEEE Symposium on Computational Intelligence in Bioinformatics and Computational Biology*, IEEE, pp. 61–66, 2004.

[SIE 89] SIEDLECKI W., SKLANSKY J., "A note on genetic algorithms for large-scale feature selection", *Pattern Recognition Letters*, vol. 10, no. 5, pp. 335–347, 1989.

[SIV 07] SIVAGAMINATHAN R.K., RAMAKRISHNAN S., "A hybrid approach for feature subset selection using neural networks and ant colony optimization", *Expert systems with applications*, Elsevier, vol. 33, no. 1, pp. 49–60, 2007.

[SKL 96] SKLANSKY J., VRIESENGA M., "Genetic selection and neural modeling of piecewise-linear classifiers", *International Journal of Pattern Recognition and Artificial Intelligence*, World Scientific, vol. 10, no. 5, pp. 587–612, 1996.

[SMY 92] SMYTH P., GOODMAN R.M., "An information theoretic approach to rule induction from databases", *IEEE Transactions on Knowledge and Data Engineering*, IEEE, vol. 4, no. 4, pp. 301–316, 1992.

[STA 13] STANIMIROVI Z., MIKOVI S., "Efficient metaheuristic approaches for exploration of online social networks", in HUW., and KAHBOUCH N. (eds), *Big Data Management Technologies, and Applications Advances in Data Mininy and Database Management, IGI Global*, 2013.

[STO 97] STORN R., PRICE K., "Differential evolution-a simple and efficient heuristic for global optimization over continuous spaces", *Journal of Global Optimization*, Springer, vol. 11, no. 4, pp. 341–359, 1997.

[STR 04] STRACUZZI D.J., UTGOFF P.E., "Randomized variable elimination", *The Journal of Machine Learning Research*, vol. 5, pp. 1331–1362, 2004.

[SUT 06] SUTTORP T., IGEL C., "Multi-objective optimization of support vector machines", in YAOCHU J. (ed.), *Multi-objective Machine Learning*, pp. 199–220, Springer, 2006.

[SUT 15] SUTHAHARAN S., *Machine Learning Models and Algorithms for Big Data Classification: Thinking with Examples for Effective Learning*, vol. 36, Springer, New York, 2015.

[TAH 04a] TAHIR M.A., BOURIDANE A., KURUGOLLU F. *et al.*, "Feature selection using Tabu search for improving the classification rate prostate needle biopsies", *Proceedings of the 17th International Conference on Pattern Recognition*, vol. 2, pp. 335–338, August 2004.

[TAH 04b] TAHIR M.A., BOURIDANE A., KURUGOLLU F., "*Proceedings of 5th International Conference on Intelligent Data Engineering and Automated Learning – IDEAL*", Chapter Simultaneous Feature Selection and Weighting for Nearest Neighbor Using Tabu Search, Springer, pp. 390–395, 2004.

[TAL 09] TALBI E.-G., *Metaheuristics: from design to implementation*, John Wiley & Sons, New York, vol. 74, 2009.

[TAL 15] TALBI E.-G., "Parallel evolutionary combinatorial optimization", KACPRZYK J., PEDRYCZ W. (eds), *Handbook of Computational Intelligence*, Springer, pp. 1107–1125, 2015.

[TAN 02] TAN P.-N., KUMAR V., SRIVASTAVA J., "Selecting the right interestingness measure for association patterns", *Proceedings of the Eight ACM SIGKDD conference, Edmonton, Canada*, 2002.

[TAN 05] TAN P., STEINBACH M., KUMAR V., *Introduction to Data Mining*, Addison-Wesley, Boston, 2005.

[TIM 10] TIMMIS J., ANDREWS P., HART E., "On artificial immune systems and swarm intelligence", *Swarm Intelligence*, Springer, vol. 4, no. 4, pp. 247–273, 2010.

[TRI 15] TRIGUERO I., PERALTA D., BACARDIT J. *et al.*, "MRPR: a MapReduce solution for prototype reduction in Big Data classification", *neurocomputing*, Elsevier, vol. 150, pp. 331–345, 2015.

[TSE 01] TSENG L., YANG S., "Genetic approach to the automatic clustering problem", *Pattern Recognition*, vol. 34, no. 2, pp. 415–424, 2001.

[TSU 13] TSUTSUI S. COLLET P. (eds), *Massively Parallel Evolutionary Computation on GPGPUs*, Springer, 2013.

[TU 07] TU C.-J., CHUANG L.-Y., CHANG J.-Y. *et al.*, "Feature selection using PSO-SVM", *International Journal of Computer Science*, vol. 33, no. 1, 2007.

[UST 11] ÜSTÜNKAR G., ÖZÖÜR-AKYÜZ S., WEBER G.W. *et al.*, "Selection of representative SNP sets for genome-wide association studies: a metaheuristic approach", *Optimization Letters*, vol. 6, no. 6, pp. 1207–1218, 2011.

[VAL 02] VALENZUELA C.L., "A simple evolutionary algorithm for multi-objective optimization (SEAMO)", *wcci*, IEEE, pp. 717–722, 2002.

[VAN 00] VAN VELDHUIZEN D.A., LAMONT G.B., "On measuring multi-objective evolutionary algorithm performance", *Proceedings of the 2000 Congress on Evolutionary Computation*, IEEE, vol. 1, pp. 204–211, 2000.

[VAN 15] VANDROMME M., JACQUES J., TAILLARD J. *et al.*, "Handling numerical data to evolve classification rules using a multi-objective local search", *Metaheuristics International Conference (MIC)*, p. 10, 2015.

[VOU 99] VOUDOURIS C., TSANG E., "Guided local search and its application to the traveling salesman problem", *European Journal of Operational Research*, Elsevier, vol. 113, no. 2, pp. 469–499, 1999.

[WAL 10] WALTON M., GREWAL G., DARLINGTON G., "Parallel FPGA-based implementation of scatter search", *Proceedings of the 12th Annual Conference on Genetic and Evolutionary Computation*, GECCO '10, ACM, pp. 1075–1082, New York, USA, 2010.

[WAN 98] WANG K., TAY S.H.W., LIU B., "Interestingness-based interval merger for numeric association rules", *KDD*, pp. 121–128, 1998.

[WAN 09] WANG Y., LI L., NI J. *et al.*, "Feature selection using Tabu search with long-term memories and probabilistic neural networks", *Pattern Recognition Letters*, Elsevier, vol. 30, no. 7, pp. 661–670, 2009.

[WAR 13] WARD J.S., BARKER A., "Undefined by data: a survey of big data definitions", *arXiv preprint arXiv:1309.5821*, 2013.

[WHI 12] WHITE D.R., "Software review: the ECJ toolkit", *Genetic Programming and Evolvable Machines*, vol. 13, no. 1, pp. 65–67, 2012.

[WIK 16a] WIKIPEDIA, "Parallel computing – Wikipedia, The Free Encyclopedia", 2016, [Online; accessed 12-May-2016].

[WIK 16b] WIKIPEDIA, "Task parallelism – Wikipedia, The Free Encyclopedia", 2016, [Online; accessed 12-May-2016].

[WIL 45] WILCOXON F., "Individual comparisons by ranking methods", *Biometrics Bulletin*, JSTOR, vol. 1, no. 6, pp. 80–83, 1945.

[WIL 04] WILSON G., MC INTYRE A., HEYWOOD M., "Resource review: three open source systems for evolving programs–Lilgp, ECJ and grammatical evolution", *Genetic Programming and Evolvable Machines*, Kluwer Academic Publishers, vol. 5, no. 1, pp. 103–105, 2004.

[WIL 11] WILLIAMS G.J., *Data Mining with Rattle and R: The art of excavating data for knowledge discovery*, Springer, New York, 2011.

[WOO 02] WOODRUFF D.L., VOSS S., *Optimization software class libraries*, Operations Research-Computer science interfaces series, Kluwer Academic Publ. corp., Boston, Dordrecht, London, 2002.

[XIA 10] XIAO J., YAN Y., ZHANG J. *et al.*, "A quantum-inspired genetic algorithm for k-means clustering", *Expert Systems with Applications*, vol. 37, no. 7, pp. 4966–4973, 2010.

[XIO 10] XIONG N., FUNK P., "Combined feature selection and similarity modeling in case-based reasoning using hierarchical memetic algorithm", *IEEE Congress on Evolutionary Computation*, IEEE, pp. 1–6, 2010.

[XU 04] XU X., CHEN L., CHEN Y., "A4C: an adaptive artificial ants clustering algorithm", *Proceedings of the 2004 IEEE Symposium on Computational Intelligence in Bioinformatics and Computational Biology*, pp. 268–275, October 2004.

[XUA 11] XUAN P., GUO M.Z., WANG J. *et al.*, "Genetic algorithm-based efficient feature selection for classification of pre-miRNAs", *Genetics and Molecular Research: GMR*, vol. 10, no. 2, pp. 588–603, 2011.

[XUE 13] XUE B., ZHANG M., BROWNE W.N., "Particle swarm optimization for feature selection in classification: a multi-objective approach", *IEEE Transactions on Cybernetics*, IEEE, vol. 43, no. 6, pp. 1656–1671, 2013.

[YAN 08] YANG C.-S., CHUANG L.-Y., CHEN Y.-J. *et al.*, "Feature selection using memetic algorithms", *Third International Conference on Convergence and Hybrid Information Technology*, vol. 1, IEEE, pp. 416–423, 2008.

[YAN 09] YAN X., ZHANG C., ZHANG S., "Genetic algorithm-based strategy for identifying association rules without specifying actual minimum support", *Expert Systems with Applications*, Elsevier, vol. 36, no. 2, pp. 3066–3076, 2009.

[YAN 13] YANG P., LIU W., ZHOU B.B. *et al.*, "Ensemble-based wrapper methods for feature selection and class imbalance learning", in JIAN P., VINCENT S., LEAIGBING C. *et al.*, (eds), *Advances in Knowledge Discovery and Data Mining*, Springer, pp. 544–555, 2013.

[YAO 05] YAO X., "A selected introduction to evolutionary computation", *Knowledge Incorporation in Evolutionary computation*, Springer, pp. 3–12, 2005.

[YE 06] YE Y., CHIANG C.-C., "A parallel Apriori algorithm for frequent item sets' mining", *Proceedings of the Fourth International Conference on Software Engineering Research, Management and Applications*, IEEE Computer Society, pp. 87–94, 2006.

[YIF 12] YIFEI ZHENG LIXIN JIA H.C., "Multi-objective gene expression programming for clustering", vol. 41, no. 3, pp. 283–294, 2012.

[ZAK 01] ZAKI M.J., "Parallel sequence mining on shared-memory machines", *Journal of Parallel and Distributed Computing*, vol. 61, no. 3, pp. 401–426, 2001.

[ZHA 00] ZHANG G.P., "Neural networks for classification: a survey", *IEEE Transactions on Systems, Man and Cybernetics, Part: C (Applications and Reviews)*, vol. 30, no. 4, pp. 451–462, November 2000.

[ZHA 02] ZHANG H., SUN G., "Feature selection using Tabu search method", *Pattern Recognition*, vol. 35, no. 3, pp. 701–711, 2002.

[ZHA 05] ZHANG P., VERMA B., KUMAR K., "Neural vs. statistical classifier in conjunction with genetic algorithm based feature selection", *Pattern Recognition Letters*, Elsevier, vol. 26, no. 7, pp. 909–919, 2005.

[ZHE 15] ZHENG B., ZHANG J., YOON S.W., *et al.*, "Predictive modeling of hospital readmissions using metaheuristics and data mining", *Expert Systems with Applications*, Elsevier, vol. 42, no. 20, pp. 7110–7120, 2015.

[ZHU 07] ZHU Z., ONG Y.-S., DASH M., "Wrapper–filter feature selection algorithm using a memetic framework", *IEEE Transactions on Systems, Man, and Cybernetics, Part B: Cybernetics*, IEEE, vol. 37, no. 1, pp. 70–76, 2007.

[ZHU 12] ZHU L., CAO L., YANG J., "Multi-objective evolutionary algorithm-based soft subspace clustering", *IEEE Congress on Evolutionary Computation*, pp. 1–8, 2012.

[ZIT 99a] ZITZLER E., *Evolutionary algorithms for multiobjective optimization: methods and applications*, Citeseer, vol. 63, 1999.

[ZIT 99b] ZITZLER E., THIELE L., "Multi-objective evolutionary algorithms: a comparative case study and the strength Pareto approach", *IEEE Transactions on Evolutionary Computation*, IEEE, vol. 3, no. 4, pp. 257–271, 1999.

[ZIT 01] ZITZLER E., LAUMANNS M., THIELE L., "SPEA2: improving the strength Pareto evolutionary algorithm", *Proceedings of the EUROGEN'2001*, Athens, Greece, 2001.

[ZIT 03] ZITZLER E., THIELE L., LAUMANNS M. *et al.*, "Performance assessment of multi-objective optimizers: an analysis and review", *IEEE Transactions on Evolutionary Computation*, IEEE, vol. 7, no. 2, pp. 117–132, 2003.

[ZIT 04] ZITZLER E., KÜNZLI S., "Indicator-based selection in multi-objective search", *Parallel Problem Solving from Nature-PPSN VIII*, Springer, pp. 832–842, 2004.

Index

Other titles from

in

Computer Engineering

2016

DEROUSSI Laurent
Metaheuristics for Logistics (Metaheuristics Set – Volume 4)

LABADIE Nacima, PRINS Christian, PRODHON Caroline
*Metaheuristics for Vehicle Routing Problems
(Metaheuristics Set – Volume 3)*

LEROY Laure
Eyestrain Reduction in Stereoscopy

MAGOULÈS Frédéric, ZHAO Hai-Xiang
Data Mining and Machine Learning in Building Energy Analysis

2015

BARBIER Franck, RECOUSSINE Jean-Luc
*COBOL Software Modernization: From Principles to Implementation with
the BLU AGE® Method*

CHEN Ken
*Performance Evaluation by Simulation and Analysis with Applications to
Computer Networks*

BOULANGER Jean-Louis
Static Analysis of Software: The Abstract Interpretation

CAFERRA Ricardo
Logic for Computer Science and Artificial Intelligence

HOMES Bernard
Fundamentals of Software Testing

KORDON Fabrice, HADDAD Serge, PAUTET Laurent, PETRUCCI Laure
Distributed Systems: Design and Algorithms

KORDON Fabrice, HADDAD Serge, PAUTET Laurent, PETRUCCI Laure
Models and Analysis in Distributed Systems

LORCA Xavier
Tree-based Graph Partitioning Constraint

TRUCHET Charlotte, ASSAYAG Gerard
Constraint Programming in Music

VICAT-BLANC PRIMET Pascale *et al.*
Computing Networks: From Cluster to Cloud Computing

2010

AUDIBERT Pierre
Mathematics for Informatics and Computer Science

BABAU Jean-Philippe *et al.*
Model Driven Engineering for Distributed Real-Time Embedded Systems 2009

BOULANGER Jean-Louis
Safety of Computer Architectures

MONMARCHE Nicolas *et al.*
Artificial Ants

PANETTO Hervé, BOUDJLIDA Nacer
Interoperability for Enterprise Software and Applications 2010

PASCHOS Vangelis Th
Combinatorial Optimization and Theoretical Computer Science: Interfaces and Perspectives

WALDNER Jean-Baptiste
Nanocomputers and Swarm Intelligence

2007

BENHAMOU Frédéric, JUSSIEN Narendra, O'SULLIVAN Barry
Trends in Constraint Programming

JUSSIEN Narendra
A to Z of Sudoku

2006

BABAU Jean-Philippe *et al.*
From MDD Concepts to Experiments and Illustrations – DRES 2006

HABRIAS Henri, FRAPPIER Marc
Software Specification Methods

MURAT Cecile, PASCHOS Vangelis Th
Probabilistic Combinatorial Optimization on Graphs

PANETTO Hervé, BOUDJLIDA Nacer
Interoperability for Enterprise Software and Applications 2006 / IFAC-IFIP I-ESA'2006

2005

GÉRARD Sébastien *et al.*
Model Driven Engineering for Distributed Real Time Embedded Systems

PANETTO Hervé
Interoperability of Enterprise Software and Applications 2005

Printed and bound by CPI Group (UK) Ltd, Croydon, CR0 4YY

27/10/2024

14580735-0002